"Stephen has quickly entrepreneurship education. His passionate, energetic approach is especially relatable and contagious throughout all his materials. As leaders engage with Stephen's content, there is no doubt they will leave motivated and better equipped with real & relevant ways in which to forge the transformative values of an entrepreneurship mindset into the educational journey of the next generation."

— Ryan Bredow, Ed.D.
Assistant Vice President, Academic Alliances K12
Educational Development
Grand Canyon University

"Stephen Carter is a brilliant yet practical thinker, truly innovative based on his innate knowledge of how things work, a proven builder of sustainable businesses and an inspiring teacher who deeply engages even the most greenhorn students. Stephen is the real deal able to teach us all about effective, inspiring, engaging and principled entrepreneurship."

— Randy Brunk
NextEd Consulting Firm
Former Head of School, Cincinnati Hills Christian Academy

"Stephen Carter has learned the secrets to student motivation, growing grit and resilience, and excitement for learning with his entrepreneurship work. Students are excited to own their learning and they love the chance to show their skills in problem-solving and teamwork."

— Tom Isaacs
Superintendent
Warren County Educational Service Center

"Stephen Carter's book on entrepreneurial mindset is a transformative guide that ignites the spark of innovation within every reader. With wisdom and clarity, Carter reveals the keys to unlocking your potential, fostering resilience, and embracing uncertainty on the path to entrepreneurial success. This book is not just a read; it's a roadmap to mastering the art of turning challenges into opportunities."

— Tawanna Rusk
Associate Head of School
Mount Paran Christian School

"Teaching entrepreneurship within the school setting is exciting for students as they are already thinking creatively and offers a space for them to channel their ideas. But the greater gain is teaching the entrepreneurship mindset. It is foundational to a student's success and easily transferable from operating a new business venture to their daily coursework and social interactions. This program is invaluable for our students and perfectly aligns to our school's mission of developing a student's character, intellect, and potential to explore, create, challenge, and lead."

— Teresa Chambers
Head of School
First Baptist Academy

"Our students are smarter than we give them credit for," writes Stephen Carter. That sums up the rationale for learning to think like an entrepreneur. It's the land of creativity, invites success and failure, develops empathy for the emotional responses of others, and provides the formula for continuous improvement. The entire transformative process is clearly spelled out in this clear and useful book."

— Joel Backon
Vice President, OESIS Network
Editor, Intrepid Ed News

To Chandler —

TEACHING
— THE —
ENTREPRENEURIAL
MINDSET

INNOVATIVE EDUCATION FOR K-12 SCHOOLS

You absolutely rock —

I loved having you in class and it has been great catching up (though it makes me feel old)!

Keep crushing it

BY STEPHEN CARTER

Romans 12:2

Copyright © 2023 by Stephen Carter
First Edition

SeedTree™
GROUP

All Rights Reserved. No part of this publication may be reproduced, distributed, or transmitted in any form or by any means, including photography, recording, or other electronic or mechanical methods, or by any information storage and retrieval system without the prior written permission of the publisher, except in the case of very brief quotations embodied in critical reviews and certain other noncommercial uses permitted by copyright law.

ISBN: 978-1-7379675-2-1

For Treva
My grandmother and lifelong cheerleader

BRING THE ENTREPRENEURIAL MINDSET TO YOUR SCHOOL

The movement is underway, it's all about engagement.

Thinking like an entrepreneur means:
Growth Mindset
Grit
Redefining Failure
Opportunity Seeking

Reach out to Stephen Carter today for speaking, consulting, and coaching services that will radically impact those in your community.

Stephen@Seedtreegroup.com
www.seedtreegroup.com

CONTENTS

FOREWORD – *Dean Nicholas*	1
Prologue	3
Introduction	7
PART ONE – *The Story*	15
Chapter One	29
Chapter Two	35
Chapter Three	51
Chapter Four	61
Chapter Five	69
Chapter Six	85
Chapter Seven	93
Chapter Eight	103
Chapter Nine	111
Chapter Ten	121
Chapter Eleven	131
Chapter Twelve	139
Chapter Thirteen	147
Chapter Fourteen	157
Chapter Fifteen	167
Chapter Sixteen	173
Chapter Seventeen	177

PART TWO – *The Attributes of the Entrepreneurial Mindset* 187

Introduction 191
Attribute One: Growth Mindset 195
Attribute Two: Grit 215
Attribute Three: Redefining Failure 239
Attribute Four: Opportunity Seeking 255
Final Charge 271
Mission, Vision, Values 281
About The Author 285
Next Steps 287

FOREWORD

Today is the first day of school. As an administrator in an academic institution, one must tend to an unending list of logistics and personnel to make sure the day goes off without a hitch. But I have an even greater concern each year as students stream into our buildings, from preschoolers to seniors. How well are we preparing our students for the world they will encounter post secondary education? And the corollary question is, to what degree are we able to engage a diverse group of learners in an age of social media reels and YouTube clips? The world is changing at an ever-increasing speed with AI, the next great disruptor. Many educators bemoan students' work ethic and fall into the old trope that students aren't what they used to be. Post-pandemic, teachers across the country are leaving the profession with a sense of hopelessness. But as a head of a private independent school, I am fortunate to work in a place of innovation and engagement, where teachers create unique opportunities for students to pursue their passions as they learn and grow in authentic ways. A prime example of such an educator is Stephen Carter.

Stephen Carter is the director of the Entrepreneurship and Sustainability Program at Cincinnati Hills Christian Academy. Stephen is what Liz Wiseman calls an "impact player," one who leads and adapts to change rather than pushing problems up the chain of command, waiting to be told what to do. The following story recounts his journey from an English teacher who took on the responsibility of a coffee bar to the leader of a program that is rethinking and reshaping how we "do school." The impact of his program is changing the opportunities and experiences of students as it propels the spirit of innovation forward in our school. It is shaping our culture and driving enrollment. In this book, Stephen does not simply suggest adding new kinds of programs and classes to schools' curricula but challenges all of us—students, teachers, and administrators—with a new way of thinking. This is not a step-by-step "how-to" book but an example of how the entrepreneurial mindset can revolutionize your classroom and your school.

I am excited for the year ahead and the new paths we can travel as educators. I know that the entrepreneurial mindset requires an openness to autonomy and taking risks. I'm not sure how our foray into *goat yoga* this year will go exactly, but even in failures, we can create unimaginable opportunities for programmatic and personal growth. I see it every day in the CHCA school culture. And as an alumni parent, I see the fruits of the program in my own child. Who knows what this year might bring? I'm open and curious for all that comes.

— Dean Nicholas, Head of School
Cincinnati Hills Christian Academy
August 16, 2023

PROLOGUE

At twenty-four years old, I was fresh off a master's degree in English from Xavier University and was teaching English 10 honors and English 12 AP Literature. I was working harder than I had ever worked in my life—staying up late grading papers while rereading *A Tale of Two Cities*—and it wasn't always easy to get to the faculty lounge by 7:30 on Wednesday mornings for a staff meeting, but I persevered. And on this particular morning, in the early fall, as the leaves were just starting to change colors and the faintest touch of chill was in the air, I hurried to my seat as one of my colleagues began to speak.

"Before I begin," he said, as teachers rushed in to take their seats, "let me pass these out."

He paused and began passing out small cards to everyone. On the card, a shirtless man sporting a chiseled physique was crouched and ready to run. His head was clean-shaven and shining with the exception of one distinct lock of long, flowing hair streaming from the front of his head and spilling over his face, partially covering his eyes.

"Meet Caerus. A son of Zeus whose distinctive hair sets him apart and often camouflages him, making him hard to notice at first. And Caerus is always on his tiptoes," he said, gesturing to the running stance in the picture. "Always ready to run, racing from place to place.

"Caerus is the god of opportunity. Some say luck, or even fortune. And when Caerus comes running your way, you have to grab him by the lock of hair in the front of face. If you wait, or pause, or even take a moment to consider, you're too late and you're left facing the back of his shiny, bald head as he runs away."

He paused to let this sink in.

"I'm not going to overdo it with the application but suffice to say, this is a personal inspiration to me. A reminder. We must always be ready, always seeking opportunity, always anticipating its arrival. Because when opportunity comes, it doesn't wait around for us to make decisions or hold meetings or conference with others. Opportunity pauses just long enough for us to recognize it and grab hold with all our might.

"Those who are ready have a shot—those who are not ready will catch only the glimpse of his shiny head as he runs off toward someone else.

"My thought for us and for the school year ahead is simple: may we recognize opportunity when it comes running and may we have the courage to grab hold of it and hang on for the ride."

The meeting then continued in its traditional form and a short while later, we left the room to enter the chaos of the everyday and the whirlwind of experience called life. But in some indefinable way, I was changed. Even now, seventeen years later as I hold up the card, weathered by age and constant handling, I remember the feeling of anticipation. Of understanding. All at once, in that morning meeting, I came face-to-face with a profound sense of meaning and purpose. I determined, then and there and for years to come, that I would constantly be in a state of preparation for Caerus. That I would tirelessly pursue opportunity and grab hold of his hair before he had a chance to run away.

The thought I was presented with that day has become the charge for myself each day since. It is now the charge I offer up to you, reader, that you may transform your life and your calling through recognizing opportunity. And that, when you do, you may move to seize it with all your might.

— Stephen Carter

INTRODUCTION

"On the first day of school, I tell them that I'm the bus driver. But then I explain that they are the GPS. They decide where we go and they establish the route. My job is to make sure the bus doesn't run off the road, but their job is to get it to the destination."

— Zachary Anderson
Associate Director of Entrepreneurship
Cincinnati Hills Christian Academy

I have labored for the last eighteen years in the domain of K–12 education. Prior to that, I grew up in a household run by an educator turned administrator. I am married to an educator, and I have teaching methodology coursing through my veins.

And I have seen the shift.

Rather than give the sense that I have a working knowledge of educational practices from the 1940s and beyond, please note that my teaching experience started in 2005 and my firsthand knowledge of the topic encompasses the last two decades of graduating seniors. But I have, nonetheless, seen a clear and undeniable shift in education. And this shift is directly connected to the *why* behind our educational model.

Visit any classroom from ten years ago (and many still operating today), or watch any pseudo-inspirational educator as hero film, and you'll be confronted with the annoyingly persistent question: "Why do we have to learn this?" Also presented in the form of "When are we ever going to use this?" this question has led many an otherwise fine teacher down the path of self-doubt and distraction.

"Because," the well-meaning teacher responds, "because you'll need this in the future."

"But when?" the student persists.

"When you get a career. This stuff is important. You'll see. It just is. Now let's turn to page 265 and complete the first ten problems."

And with that seemingly simple response, the teacher just lost all credibility in the eyes of the students. This is the hard truth that we as educators all subconsciously know and yet often fail to recognize—our students are smarter than we give them credit for. Yes, even that one student you're now thinking of, sitting in the corner, and scoffing at 80 percent of everything you say, even she is smarter than we give her credit for. And they know—they know what is of value and what is not. They know what will help them build a successful future and what will not. And they know when they are being duped.

Lest you immediately dismiss me and write me off as a contrarian who wants to undermine the very nature of traditional education and core classes, please understand my intention: student engagement. When I first started as a high school English teacher, I was tasked with teaching sophomore students and more specifically with teaching them to read and analyze archaic works of literature before writing eloquently on thematic issues from the texts. From George Eliot's *Silas Marner* to Sophocles's *Oedipus*

Rex, these students were encouraged to read beyond the ancient words to find meaning through a deeper understanding of the human experience.

And it was valuable because I believed it was valuable. I worked, harder than I ever imagined possible, at convincing sixteen-year-old adolescents that there was intent and purpose behind their assignments. That there was a *why* that would help them establish a level of success and meaning in their life. I was, in other words, prepared for the question, for the smirk, for the challenge, and I offered an oratorical response that shut off all opposition and positioned me as the quintessential sage on the stage who could wax eloquent for the full forty-eight minutes on themes of loss, hope, sorrow, and redemption.

But here's my point—I faced contention. Yes, I was ready for it, yes, I steeled myself against it, but the contention was there nonetheless, and I accepted it as the cost of being an educator. I comforted myself with the knowledge that we all, collectively, face the same opposition day in and day out and it is our job to root it out of our students and awaken them to the sheer blessing that an education steeped in traditional methods can provide.

And then, one day, everything changed.

Three years into my shift from the English classroom to the world of entrepreneurship education, a story I will unfold and develop throughout this book, I came to a stark and sudden realization—*engaged students no longer asked the question.*

Please understand—it is not that they no longer questioned in general. In fact, they questioned and wondered and asked more than ever before. But what they didn't do, and what struck me in such a profound manner, is they no longer asked, "Why are we learning this?" In other words, they already knew the answer. In other words, the *why* was clear, tangible, and direct. And they knew, without my having to say, that the content was of value.

For the last ten years, we have worked to build a successful and world-class entrepreneurship program at Cincinnati Hills Christian Academy. The program currently has fifteen elective courses, a full-certificate track, and features six student-run businesses. We've woven aspects of balance and mindfulness into the curriculum and experiences to help students better equip themselves for lives of health and wellness. We send students into internships in the community and have developed a robust curriculum based on the entrepreneurial mindset. In building this program we discovered, quite by accident, a key to actively engaging this current generation of students. We discovered a methodology of education that works and that has ripple effects far beyond any specific business or elective course. We latched on to a core set of teaching practices that not only sets students up for future success regardless the industry or ever-changing future technologies, but also that they intuitively know is worthwhile and are grateful to receive.

It is worth noting that, despite using the word *entrepreneurship*, our program is focused less on creating young entrepreneurs and more on helping students *think* like entrepreneurs. Entrepreneurs are visionary problem solvers and hard-working integrators. Entrepreneurs think creatively and act resiliently. Entrepreneurs are growth-focused, gritty opportunity seekers who have redefined the definition of failure.

Consider the following story as an illustration:

Early in the fall of 2022, I was walking through our four-thousand-square-foot greenhouse situated in the center of our campus and admiring the baby tomato plants that were just beginning to be trellised on our vertical growing system (this greenhouse, like many other spaces on our campus, is run and operated by the entrepreneurship program students). As I meandered down the rows, careful to avoid tangling the lines reaching to the windowed ceilings, I heard a student call out my name.

"Mr. Carter!"

I looked up and saw the smiling face of John who just recently had taken on the role of greenhouse production manager.

"John," I said, "good to see you. How was your summer?"

"Great," he said. "And I wanted to thank you."

"Thank me?" I asked. "What for?"

Typically, when students offered up a thank you it was a coerced response to my writing a recommendation letter or allowing a late assignment to be accepted for partial credit.

"For the class last semester. On entrepreneurship."

The course John was referring to is our Foundations of Entrepreneurship course, which instead of dealing with the ins and outs of running a business, begins with a deep dive into habit formation and goal setting. It is essentially the class that introduces students to what we call the "entrepreneurial mindset." Traditionally the course fills up and has a healthy waiting list.

"You enjoyed it?" I asked.

"Immensely," he said, "but more importantly, I've been doing a lot of the things we talked about. Like with habits—I've been working on my habits and habit stacking and have really started seeing great improvements. I have a high return habit I do every day and I track my habits to form new ones. It's that compound interest thing you talked about. It made me start an investment account so I can work on earning it. Oh, and I've got goals for the year. And they're actually written down."

"That's awesome, John," I said. "I'd love to hear those goals at some point."

"Sure thing," he said. "Thanks again!"

With that, John was off to check on the kale seedlings for our aeroponic grow towers while I was left to reflect. Here was a high school senior who, as a junior, had sat through a single semester class meant to introduce the entrepreneurial mindset—meant to help students begin to develop a growth mindset, grit, the ability to redefine failure, and a desire to be opportunity seeking. And he got it: the content was having a dramatically positive effect on his life.

In the end, this is our goal as educators. We have accepted a calling. We are not merely doing "work" or even pursuing a "career," but we are embracing something larger and more important. We are charged with effecting positive change in the lives of the students we come across. Somewhere along the line, many of us give in to the numerous frustrations brought about by traditional teaching methods. Assessments seem lackluster, students are disengaged, and parents have unrealistic demands. The calling starts to feel like work and work, in this sense, can be entirely draining.

This does not have to be the case.

Our calling can and will be a rewarding one and that fills us with energy and passion and purpose. I have discovered this firsthand, over the last ten years, in helping countless students (and teachers and administrators and business owners) develop the entrepreneurial mindset. I have seen the radical transformation this shift in mindset effects in those who truly adopt it. And I am charged with sharing it with everyone I come into contact with. But don't just take my word for it. The pages of this book detail experiences, stories, suggestions, and examples of how this ideological shift in education goes far beyond innovative programming and flash-in-the-pan projects. This is about changing not just what we teach but *why* we teach. If we are going to teach the entrepreneurial mindset, we must start by embodying it ourselves. Over the past ten years, the entrepreneurship program has grown due to its two primary measures of success: student engagement and excellence in presentation. The story that unfolds in this book is one of striving ceaselessly for these measures of success—sometimes hitting them, sometimes not, but always striving. And in many ways, that is the point of this story.

— Stephen Carter
Fall, 2023

PART ONE
THE STORY

"The entrepreneurship program changed my vision in life. It motivated me to be goal driven and taught me efficient ways and skills in which I could achieve those goals, including teamwork, marketing, brainstorming, budgeting, financial literacy, and so on. I have now decided to minor in entrepreneurship in college as I start my freshman year at Grand Canyon University in fall, 2023."

— Marce, '23

Much has been written about education and the need for transformational change. Every year, schools around the nation set aside multiple days for teacher in-service where they talk about the efficacy of grading methods, the shift to reach all learners, and the use of technology in the classroom. There is even regular conversation around teaching students how to think, fostered by the belief that equipping them with this ability ensures a lifetime of success.

All of this is well and good—schools need to be willing to adapt and change and grow with the times. In-service and professional development can certainly be a productive value-add for a school and if we can reach more learners, we can be more effective. The issue stems not from these well-intentioned workshops but rather from the lack of addressing the key problem. Trying to adjust and change teaching methods in a faculty is, even if possible, merely a band-aid covering a gaping wound. And that gaping wound comes back to mindset. For years now, schools have been touting critical thinking as the primary goal of education. From the early days of Socratic dialogues to the more recent introductions of programs like Harkness, critical thinking has been lauded as the be-all and end-all of education. And I am not here to dispute that. What I am here to dispute is the ideology underlying the assumption that training in critical thinking leads to greater academic success.

I base my dispute on one primary factor: the classroom teacher. If we stop to consider the dozens and dozens of teachers we've had throughout our life, chances are a few rise to the top as highly influential. Chances are even better, however, that the vast majority have fallen out of our memory due to a lack of meaningful impact. Many of these teachers, now long forgotten, believed strongly in critical thinking and dynamic educational methods, yet they were unable to make a profound impression on us. No teacher sets out to be mediocre. In an idealistic sense, the majority of teachers set out into the profession because they believe in making an impact on future generations and sharing the joy of learning that they themselves have fostered over their lives. Despite the best of intentions, many teachers succumb to the mind-numbing realities of the job and begin to slip, ever so slowly, into a pattern of "might have been." It is the nature of the job. One enters a profession whose highest tangible rewards stem from lifelong impact and positive change and yet that impact and positive change comes, if at all, so late that its motivating power is weakened by time. The tenth-grade student who so enjoyed the teacher's class will, if he ever does at all, wait until he is in his mid-thirties before tracking them down to tell them about the impact they had. This means the dynamic, engaging teacher who is changing lives has to wait about fifteen years before seeing the fruits of her labor and feeling the satisfaction that comes from engaging in meaningful purpose.

Statistics tell us that around 40 percent of teachers leave the profession within five years. This means that even if they hit it out of the park in their classroom, they will most likely lose steam and give up a full two decades before reassurance of their impact is provided. The remaining 60 percent, it is safe to say, will be beset by the plague of paperwork, grading, parent emails, and staff meetings to the point where, by the time they hear back from their students, they have already slipped into the all-to-common malaise of educational despond. OK, you're saying, the picture is bleak. And yes, it is. But this is where the exciting path ahead is introduced. What I am suggesting is not a complete overhaul of the entire educational system (actually, the truth is, I am, but I just don't want to lead with that). What I *am* suggesting is that instead of focusing so much on the student experience and what our students are learning and how our students are thinking, let's shift the focus to our teachers. After all, a school is only as good as the teachers—they are the movers and shakers, the boots on the ground, the medics in the field, the life-changers, and the hope-givers. Instead of worrying so much about our students, let's focus on our teachers.

And when it comes to helping our teachers, what better way than to help them learn how to adjust their mindset. OK, I can see I've lost a few readers already. "How demeaning," you may be saying. "How offensive to suggest that our teachers don't know how to think." I am not suggesting that we teach them how to process and how to understand, nor am I suggesting that we break out the discussion tables and engage in critical thinking exercises. Rather, I am suggesting that we help our teachers develop the skills to think like entrepreneurs. "Like entrepreneurs," you say with skepticism. "But they aren't entrepreneurs, they are educators." Agreed. But I intend to argue, throughout this book, that those who think like entrepreneurs, in other words those who are able to look at life through a lens of growth mindset, who are able to apply grit to all situations, who are able to take risks because they've redefined failure, and those who are able to seek opportunity in all situations will not only experience tremendous success in all efforts but will effectively change the world.

Now do I have your attention? The bulk of this book will focus on how to infuse these mindset attributes into the lives of our students, but this will only work if those in the classroom are themselves proficient in this way of thinking. After all, how can we teach growth mindset if we ourselves are laboring away in a fixed mindset? How can we encourage students to apply grit if we are frustrated and want to give up? How can we suggest students take risks if we ourselves are afraid to try something new after all these years of doing the same thing? How can we say "seek opportunity" if we spend our evenings binge-watching television? The only way we can effectively teach the entrepreneurial mindset to our students is if we, as the faculty of the school, choose to adopt and demonstrate the mindset in our own lives—it truly does start at the top.

I'm regularly asked to consult with schools in starting entrepreneurship programming and these schools often want to jump right in with innovative experiences and Instagram-worthy projects. After all, they want to engage their students and win over their parents, so the flashier the start, the better. What I explain, usually to their chagrin, is that these opportunities are the by-product of the stellar entrepreneurial program—the primary engine for this comes from an administrative outlook that, by nature of influence, trickles down to the staff and faculty. After all, how can we encourage students to think like entrepreneurs if their teachers are worn down from the frustration of educational bureaucracy? How can we champion our cause if our frontline representatives hear nothing but "no" or "there's no room in the budget" or "let's table this for later." One question for administrators to ask themselves, when they're feeling like they're up for a dose of honest feedback, is whether or not their teachers would identify them as having a growth mindset. If I sat in a room with them behind closed doors, what would they say about the leadership style at the school?

It is the job of administrators to demonstrate growth mindset to the school. As John Maxwell's "Law of the Lid" suggests, an organization can only rise to the level the leader has placed upon it. If the primary role of the administrator is putting out fires and dealing with crises, then the role acts as more of a wet blanket that will smother not only fires but also potential sparks. These sparks are what we should be cultivating and encouraging. We should encourage our teachers to try new things even if it means they will fail from time to time. We should encourage them to get outside of the classroom and engage their students in different styles of learning. We should give them the room in the budget to do something totally original. If we believe in the importance of the growth mindset, our teachers will begin to believe as well. Some who read this will be tempted to think, "Well I have a growth mindset but it's just my teachers who don't. How do I get them to come on board?" And to that, I suggest two things: First, spend more time reflecting on your own growth mindset status—chances are you have some tough love to give yourself on this subject. Second, you're probably right that your teachers don't. But the key is, some of them *want* to. They *desire* it. And you need to give those teachers the freedom to move toward the growth mindset even if it means grumbling from the fixed-mindset faculty.

Much has been written about these fixed mindset teachers—the ones who occupy the far back seats in the bus in many a metaphor. The truth is, these teachers will grumble and complain regardless, but our concern needs to shift from attempting to appease these teachers (who, by the way, will *never* be appeased) to empowering the ones who desire growth. Liz Wiseman refers to these growth-desiring individuals as "Impact Players." Seth Godin calls them "Linchpins." Ron Clark calls them "Runners." Some organizations refer to them as "intrapreneurs." Regardless, once they identify themselves as individuals desiring growth, they need to be given support. Continuous application of a growth mindset is painful and difficult and requires grit, and as a result, a desire for growth should be rewarded. How can we reward a teacher's desire for growth? I'm glad you asked—with *freedom, autonomy,* and *resources.*

Freedom and trust go together. Creating an environment where freedom flourishes is certainly no easy task—it often involves allowing people to experience failure knowing that they will not be punished as a result. If a teacher sees a colleague try something new that backfires and then ends up in a conversation with administration, the wet blanket of restriction will fall over the department and eventually over the school. If a parent calls in to complain and the teacher is immediately thrown under the bus, freedom is thereby restricted. You'll notice, as we break down not only the necessity of freedom but also the means of creating an environment that encourages it, it hinges on the inherent quality of the teacher. For instance, encouraging freedom does not mean that we want our teachers to stop teaching in the middle of class, dismiss the students, and then sit back and watch YouTube videos. Or to completely throw away assessments without replacing them with something engaging and innovative. All schools have teachers who would take advantage of the system if given enough leeway—and this is sometimes the collateral damage we must endure to support the teachers who are truly bringing innovative learning to the students. The key is to shrewdly identify the teachers who are creating value and to support them publicly.

Now you're probably looking at that and thinking, "If I give certain teachers public praise, then everyone else is going to be on me to give them public praise and then I've also made a target out of those teachers." True on both fronts—but you've also done something intensely important—you've set a standard. You've said, without saying it, "This is what we have here at our school, and this is what we, as administrators, will get behind. This is the definition of innovation." There will, of course, be grumbling, but the grumbling will come from those who are either scared of, or perhaps incapable of, innovation. If they are scared, then a clear example of success may be what they need. If they are incapable, then the public praise piece doesn't matter anyway. The point is it will encourage others—the early adopters of the environment of freedom you are crafting will go all in and will set the stage for the next wave of teachers, those who are sitting back to see how the trailblazers fare. When they see the trailblazers getting the full support of administration, it will be just the impetus they need to venture out and try new things. That's the thing about freedom—it's contagious and while there will be naysayers (and prepare yourself, they will be among your most seasoned educators with parent rapport) the important thing to keep in mind is that student experience is paramount. In the end, it is the students' enthusiasm that will drive change and when we tap into that, we are reaching learning at its inner core.

Once a culture of freedom is established (and know that it takes time to build the necessary trust around freedom), it is time to begin infusing it with autonomy. As an administrator, your desire to hear about and approve every project is natural to your role. If something is going on in the school, you want to be in the know—the last thing you want is for a parent to ask about a special project and have you caught blind. And yet, for the spirit of the entrepreneurial mindset to take off, we must relinquish a portion of that control. Autonomy can only exist where there is freedom and, in reverse, true freedom requires autonomy. In a school setting, this means that a teacher needs to be free to act on an idea but also should not have to run each idea by an administrator. There will still be plenty of times when administrator buy-in will be necessary—for instance if an idea involves any form of construction on school property. I am certainly not advocating that teachers be allowed to do whatever, whenever, wherever. I am also not advocating autonomy for *all* teachers. As your program develops, the teachers who have a growth mindset will slowly trickle to the top and begin dabbling in the new model. It is these teachers who should be given the clear message of autonomy. It is these teachers who will show what's possible in your school environment.

If you give autonomy to the naysayers and lazy teachers, they are just going to use that autonomy to cancel class and head to a coffee shop to check Facebook. But don't let your fear of this happening stop you from giving the freedom and autonomy to the ones who can and will make a difference in the school. A great way to instill this autonomy is by affirming and encouraging the teacher wanting to branch out and try something new and then articulating that they don't have to come ask you every time in the future. Clarify that you would love to hear after the fact and get a summation of how it went, but that they are cleared to act of their own volition. A side effect of this mentality is a sense of ownership. As I work with schools, one of the primary attributes they want to see students develop in an entrepreneurial program is ownership, yet so often they are quick to strip any possibility of ownership away from their teachers. Once again, if we want to see an attribute in our students, we must first look to build it (or bring it out) in our teachers. If teachers feel ownership over their classroom and, by extension, over the school, they will by necessity feel a greater sense of pride. This will have all sorts of additional benefits like refusing to take part in complaining circles (that's *my* school you're talking about) and going above and beyond on a regular basis. We all would love to have hallways filled with teachers (and students) who take greater ownership and pride in the school, yet we stifle the ability when we curb freedom and autonomy.

The last necessity is resources. Ironically this is the easiest and most difficult. The easiest, because what better way to justify a use of school funds than to invest it in a project that, on a cost-benefit scale, can create student engagement? The most difficult because, as with any school, funds are limited (and, most likely, already allocated). Here's the tipping point—your entrepreneurial-minded teachers need the resources *more* than the naysaying, complaining teachers. Yes, I said that correctly. Consider the famous biblical parable of the talents—when the master returned, the talent was taken *from* the servant who buried it and did nothing with it and given *to* the servant who had wisely invested it. We are called to be good stewards of our resources, and this does not mean burying them in the ground because it's the way we've always done it.

Yes, we need to pay the electric bill and make key upgrades to our facilities. Yes, we need cleaning tools and office supplies. We need the foundational resources to keep the school running. But, and this is key, we don't have to continue to operate the way we've always operated if we are going to adopt an entrepreneurial mindset. Consider how much money your school spends on textbooks—astronomical, most likely. And those textbooks are replaced every few years with a newer edition. If we ask, most teachers and administrators would say the textbooks are necessary for student learning and that student learning is, of course, the foundational pillar on which the school is built. And yet we ignore the fact (yes, the *fact*) that no student in the history of education has ever had a life-changing moment derived from a twenty-five-pound book written in the driest possible manner. The only thing we know for sure about these textbooks is that they directly contribute to poor posture and spinal issues from being carried all over the place.

There are, of course, myriad things to consider when it comes to the school budget and I realize I am at risk of sounding simplistic, but consider the inherent question of why we are allocating funds to buy physical books when we live in an age of audiobooks, e-books, and Google? What if there was a way for this money to be reallocated to a department innovation fund where teachers can apply (in a noncomplicated manner) to receive funding for a creative student-engaged project? What if we held competitions (complete with prizes) for the most engaging interdepartmental project? What if we were celebrating the outside-the-box thinkers among our faculty and supporting them with the funding they need to continue knocking it out of the park? When I hear schools say that there's no money for these sorts of projects, I see it as a challenge—I begin to wonder if, after reviewing their budget, it would be possible to find enough money to reallocate to not only fund all these proposed projects but also dramatically increase student engagement.

This brings us to revenue streams. Let's free ourselves from the model that requires the budget to be covered entirely by tuition or by tuition and an annual fund. Revenue streams will be the funding of the future for independent schools and to create a sustainable path toward innovative education, we must think differently about how we fund our programs. When we create opportunities that allow for money to flow back in, we create opportunities for more projects of that type which, in turn, brings more money back in. Does that mean we should prioritize innovative projects that have revenue streams over innovative ideas that don't? Absolutely. If an innovative idea comes with a baked-in potential for revenue, that idea shoots to the top of the list. Otherwise, it is just a creative way to spend money. Remember, the ultimate goal is for our students to adopt the entrepreneurial mindset, and this is more likely to happen when their teachers demonstrate that mindset in real time. The entrepreneurial mindset, while rooted in growth mindset, grit, redefining failure, and opportunity seeking, is also about sustainability. This sustainability comes in the form of focus on people (balance and wellness), planet (stewardship of resources), and finally, profit (financial sustainability). If we are to think like entrepreneurs, we must create the problem-solving ideas that themselves have the potential to generate revenue.

This requires a bit of thought for the teacher planning the event, but if it becomes ingrained in the culture, then this way of thinking becomes second nature. What are the opportunities for sponsorship by local businesses? Can tickets be sold? Are prototypes being created that would have a purchasing audience? We live in a day and age where revenue streams abound, and we should be teaching our teachers, and therefore our students, to take advantage of this. If for no other reason than that the idea will become self-sustaining and not require a piece of the school budget year after year. And while the model is immediately beneficial to the school (more money coming in), the learning that is taking place has an even higher return on investment.

In the end, it may be a pipe dream to imagine an entire faculty thinking and acting like entrepreneurs. It may be too much of a stretch to push your entire staff in this direction. But is it not possible for one or two teachers to take the lead? For these one or two to then inspire another few to step in? For this cohort to then create an onboarding plan for new hires that infuses this ideology into the employment process based on core values? To then hire not just for qualification and experience but also for the mindset attributes based on these values? I'm not talking about transforming an entire organization overnight but rather creating the environment where a spark does not die out for lack of fuel but is given the necessary components (in the form of freedom, autonomy, and resources) to grow into a flame and then that flame to grow into a fire and then that fire to blaze with energy, warming everyone around. Just like this fire, the passion around the entrepreneurial mindset is contagious: it is impossible to not get excited when you see the results of this way of thinking.

Lest you think these are empty words, please know that we've lived this experience at Cincinnati Hills Christian Academy. Over the last ten years, we've built a program that has created unsurpassed engagement that encourages students to take this leap in thinking and to move toward redefining failure because they see it modeled, every day, by faculty at the school. Every single one of our entrepreneurship classes is an elective—despite it not being a graduation requirement, students sign up in droves.

We have waiting lists and applications. We have customer-centric programming that is designed to create immediate value for our students with as little waste as possible. We teach our students to think with the entrepreneurial mindset by demonstrating it ourselves. Have we completely arrived? Of course not. Like the growth mindset, it requires continuous improvement and learning and pivoting. But are we better off now than we were ten years ago? Without a doubt—and thanks to the flames of innovation, the future is bright indeed.

CHAPTER ONE

"If I'm being honest, starting to work at the coffee bar was never about entrepreneurship—I wanted free drinks and to make some friends. But through four years in the program, I learned more about problem-solving and the grit it takes to find solutions than I ever imagined I would. Rather than turn away from failure, the entrepreneurship program taught me to learn from it, and see it as an opportunity for growth."

— Patrick, '21

Perhaps it is inherent in the DNA of educators to say yes to far too many extra obligations. Perhaps it is just human nature. Regardless, in the spring of 2015, in addition to a full teaching load, I was coaching the varsity cross-country team, leading a thriving debate club bent on going to state, and planning a two-week cultural learning experience to Australia. Also worth mentioning is the fact that my wife and I had just expanded our family two months prior by welcoming our second child into our carefully controlled chaos. I had taken the lessons of grabbing the hair of Caerus to heart and was pursuing every opportunity that came my way.

And perhaps because of that attitude, opportunities constantly came my way.

"I think you'd be perfect for it," said Dean Nicholas, lovingly referred to as "Dr. Nick" by the students. Dean was currently in his eighth year as principal of the high school and had previously been the chair of the Christian Studies Department. "I want you to seriously consider it."

The "it" he was referring to was the school's coffee cart, which had started two years before. Comprised of three rolling stands, a mobile espresso machine, several insulated coffee containers, and an array of drink-making accessories, it had been an educational experiment meant to test whether or not students enjoyed the experience of running a business. Turns out, they did. In its first year, the coffee cart, named The Leaning Eagle, brought in $3,000 in gross sales and largely outperformed expectations. The three-part setup was rolled out to football games and in various parts of the school building during the day, which then added an element of fun and liveliness to the student experience. In its second year, the cart continued to thrive but also faced a few problems. Because of the nature of the setup and the way in which students circulated in and out from behind the bar, the sales remained the same while the number of drinks made skyrocketed. In short, students were treating the coffee cart like their own personal barista service where they could make free drinks for themselves and their friends.

They lacked a sense of ownership.

It was at this point, several weeks after the teacher overseeing the cart had announced his departure from the school, that I found myself sitting down with Dean to discuss the future of the venture.

"I'm not sure," I said, hesitantly.

"The program needs someone like you to oversee it," he said.

"Oh, I'm definitely interested," I said, "but I currently have a lot of things on my plate."

"Which is exactly why I'm asking you. Look at everything you are doing and have done here at the school. You bring a level of excellence and that's exactly what I need from this project."

Like most people, I'm a sucker for flattery. It also helped that I am mildly obsessed with single origin coffee, perfect pour-overs, and exquisite latte art. I could almost see Caerus preparing to run by and knew that I should start reaching for him.

"Would it be the sort of thing where I could make decisions and bring changes?" I asked.

"Change away—I am asking you because I *want* you to make the changes you see fit," he said.

"I'm talking about some big changes," I said.

"The bigger the better," he said.

"So, you're saying I have your permission," I said.

"Just show me the plan and we will make it happen," he said.

It is at this point in the story that I feel it necessary to insert the following caveat to my readers. One of the reasons I have enjoyed such a long tenure at Cincinnati Hills Christian Academy (currently in year seventeen) is because of the school's approach to ideation. Since my first year, whenever I approached my administration with an idea or plan or proposal, I never received an immediate refusal. More often than not, I was given a yes, a go-ahead, or a let's see how it plays out. As the rest of this book will demonstrate, this atmosphere is essential for developing the entrepreneurial mindset. Even in these early days, without my knowing it, I was being primed to think like an entrepreneur—

encouraged to come up with an idea, possibly fail, learn from the failure, and adapt and grow in amazing ways.

This was true both in and out of the classroom. We were always encouraged to try new things and branch out into the unfamiliar. At one point this meant allowing my AP English Literature students to heave their copies of Chaucer's *Canterbury Tales* to the side in favor of a walk around the campus grounds while acting out the book by telling individual stories. That particular experiment was a huge success, but not all of the experiments took off. One epic failure began when I tried to play out a deserted island scenario in the classroom to set the stage for *Lord of the Flies*. After informing the students of the plane crash and that I was "not present," they proceeded to trash the classroom, ruin four textbooks, and disgruntle at least eight of my colleagues. Ironically, though, this failed experiment did demonstrate human depravity in a way that set the stage for Golding's work. The point is that I never had to fear chastisement for trying. If anything, the mentality was if you don't try, then you never know.

This is why, when Dean gave me permission to make big changes to the current coffee cart, I started to dream. And I dreamed big. But neither Dean nor I came close to dreaming of how big this project would eventually become.

Step one was to assemble a team of students. This involved roaming the school, sharing the vision with any who would listen. My pitch to them had eerily similar aspects to the famous (and possibly mythical) ad run by Ernest Shackleton in seeking men for his Antarctica expedition. Shackleton is said to have posted the following:

WANTED: MEN FOR HAZARDOUS JOURNEY. SMALL WAGES, BITTER COLD, LONG MONTHS OF COMPLETE DARKNESS, CONSTANT DANGER, SAFE RETURN DOUBTFUL. HONOR AND RECOGNITION IN CASE OF SUCCESS.

It is said that he received thousands of responses to this and that he went out of his way to not sugarcoat the overall experience. Although I was dealing with a coffee cart and not a voyage to the south pole, the tone needed to be similar:

WANTED: STUDENTS FOR DIFFICULT PROJECT. NO WAGES, LONG HOURS, HARD WORK FROM START TO FINISH, POTENTIAL FOR FAILURE, NO GUARANTEE OF SUCCESS. ABILITY TO BE PART OF SOMETHING AMAZING.

It has been debated whether or not Shackleton's ad really existed and whether or not it actually garnered the thousands of responses reported. Regardless, I can definitively say that when I tried a similar selling technique, the team filled up instantly. There is certainly something to be said about the allure of difficulty and the need to apply grit (alongside blood, sweat, and tears). There's something to be said about offering a challenge to a society that has largely grown up sheltered from hard work and discipline. There's something to be said about stepping off into the unknown to forge a new path—the appeal is undeniable.

And so, with a full team of students, actively engaged and fueled by a wealth of dreams, the brainstorming began.

CHAPTER TWO

"The entrepreneurship program challenged me to intertwine creativity and logic to design a dream that was realistic yet impactful. I still find myself tapping regularly into the research, critical thinking, and management skills gained from this experience."

— Gianna, '21

The students were enlisted to begin market research—or at least that's the fancy term we now use. What really happened was we dove headfirst into learning everything we could about coffee. Where it was shipped from, how much it cost, who roasted it, how was it best prepared. From there, we began traveling to local coffee shops to take pictures, sample drinks, and learn the layout. We spoke with local roasters and learned all about our equipment needs. All along, we continued to dream.

The next phase involved conducting student interviews. We wanted to know what was working well with the existing coffee cart and what students wanted to change. We interviewed teachers on their frustrations (later we would call these "pain points") and worked to learn what would help solve their problems. And through these discussions, it became apparent that we would need to flip the existing model of the business.

Primarily, this meant moving from a mobile cart into a permanent location—a move that would allow us to expand our footprint, which would allow for more equipment and a larger menu. It also meant we could really apply some of what we had seen at the local shops around town.

Location scouting began and we looked at the current concessions space near our gymnasium, at a vacated classroom turned storage room, and inside the current library. None of the locations seemed just right and none seemed to offer the "feel" we were going for. Back to the drawing board, we began to look at where the current mobile cart had been most successful. Since it could be rolled anywhere, it had operated in most areas of the school but the one location that drew the most attention was when it was set up directly in the middle of our commons area. Dubbed "Miracle Commons" after a beloved principal, Joan Miracle, this space is a large, open foyer that leads to all the classrooms as well as the administrative offices. It is the first place visitors see upon entering and it is the primary entrance for all students. And it was perfect for a permanent coffee shop.

This, of course, brought about the realization that our work had just begun. We had to get approval for building in the space, figure out how much the build-out would cost, determine a way to get the funding, hire the necessary people to do the work, purchase the additional equipment, find reputable suppliers, train the student managers, and operate a successful business. And to top it all off, we wanted this to be up and running by the start of the next school year, which gave us a solid three months.

It is at this point in the story that it is worth diverting to explain an essential philosophy that has been applied since the inception of our entrepreneurship program: When in doubt, act. Take action. Don't sit around and wait, letting Caerus pass by. Get up and *do*. Those who know me know that I have several key pet peeves but perhaps the most significant one is toward those who talk but never do. Talking and planning and thinking and brainstorming make up only a small portion of the task—it is in the doing where we embrace our entrepreneurial spirit. And it is essential that our innovative programming operates with this philosophy.

In order to *do*, we needed money, and therefore the project started the way most of our future ventures would also start—by going to Dean Nicholas and asking for money. I thought it best to go alone to the meeting and to report back to the students.

"So how is the planning going?" Dean asked.

"It is going great—we're excited and have a great team. And we have some amazing plans that you will love—I don't want to spoil it but let's just say that we are going to build a permanent location for The Leaning Eagle. And it will only cost $50,000," I said.

"I'm listening," said Dr. Nick.

"Picture this," I said, spreading my arms wide. "You walk into Miracle Commons and are immediately hit with the amazing smell of perfectly roasted coffee. You turn and see CHCA students operating a bustling business and serving amazing drinks. The entire school seems alive with energy and passion."

"And it costs $50,000?" he asked, skeptically.

"We're going to build a permanent location for the coffee cart and call it a 'coffee bar.' We're going to need electric, plumbing, construction, everything. We need to buy new equipment and really blow this thing out of the water. And we need the money to do it."

"Sounds like you've got your vision. Now I just need a plan."

"As in different from what I just told you?" I asked.

"A business plan," he said. "I want everything laid out, explained, and justified. Then we can talk potential funding."

I called the team of students together to share this news. None of us, myself included, knew how to make a business plan or had any experience with business plans, but a few simple Google searches turned up all we needed to know and more. This concept, by the way, became an ongoing philosophy throughout the growth and development of the program over the years. As long as we leaned toward action rather than inaction, we usually ended up ahead. In this particular scenario, our team divided the primary sections of the plan and got down to business. Within two weeks, we had a decent draft drawn up and a specific cost narrowed down—we also felt confident that just as we had never encountered a business plan before, there was a good chance that the school administration team also did not regularly encounter them, so we were able to wing it if we had to.

"Looks good," said Dean, looking over the pages of projections and market opportunity. "Impressive and ambitious. Now, in terms of funding—"

"Just $45,000," I said. "Less than last time. A bargain, really."

"Certainly sounds like it," he said. "But we're going to go a different route."

"Different route?" I said. "What sort of different route?"

"I want you to treat this like an actual business. With an actual business, you don't just get money to start. You take out a loan. I'm proposing you take out a loan for the coffee bar."

"A loan?" Images of creditors and loan sharks loomed over me.

"A loan, yes, but not from a bank. From the school. From our business office. I talked with them and they are going to let you take out an interest-free loan that the coffee bar has to pay back within three years."

I was crestfallen. We had put together a business plan to grow an idea that Dean himself had asked me to take on and rather than give me the funding for the project, he was suggesting we had to create a plan to pay it back. My expression must not have fully betrayed my emotion because Dean continued with even more devastating news.

"And the amount will be a bit less. The loan will be for $10,000."

"Only $10,000? But we projected $45,000."

"I'm going to give you $5,000 out of the high school budget to pay for the electric you need, but other than that, you're going to get $10,000 and whatever is left in the current account."

The current account, to my knowledge, had just over $4,000 in it, so this left us with $19,000 or less than half of our projected cost. Now my face must have betrayed my frustration. I had been expecting the easy route of getting a lump sum financial gift from the school and moving forward. A loan required payments, which required sales, which required success, and added a whole new element of reality to the project. This was no longer just a side project—it was a business that *had* to work.

"Think of this as a learning experience for the students," he said. "And, perhaps, for you."

"What happens if we can't pay it back?" I asked.

"That doesn't sound like you," he said, smiling. "Don't forget that I picked you out for this opportunity. And there's a reason I did."

"OK," I said, shifting gears mid-conversation. I could see Caerus lacing up his shoes in the distance. "I want to rephrase that last comment. What I meant to say was, what happens if we pay it off early?"

"That's more like it," he said. "I'll reach out to the business office and get this settled and you can start right away."

And just like that, we dove in. And by dove in, I mean fully in, immersed in the experience of building a business from the ground up. That summer, which was anything but a typical summer, was spent with contractors, plumbers, electricians, and suppliers. Looking back, this is where some of the greatest learning experiences of the entire program originated, but at the time, it was a daily uphill grind with little to no chance of success. "Winging it" barely describes the way we operated. There were many a night where I was cradling my newborn son in one arm and wielding a laptop with the other, trying to finalize a logo while picking out stain colors while deciding on apron designs. That summer I was part-contractor, part-electrician, part-plumber, part-barista, part-interior designer. And no parts were played with ease.

Perhaps the greatest benefit of the process was the enforced creativity. Because of the limited funds, we had to act with extreme frugality regarding all aspects of the build. When we were informed by the plumbing company that the cost to run water and a drain line for a new sink at our chosen location would be north of $18,000, we quickly reconvened to look at our options.

"How important is having a sink?" one student asked.

"Nonnegotiable," I said. I had just gotten off the phone with the county health inspector after discovering that our operation would now require an official health license, which required a litany of additional steps.

"Well $18,000 is almost our entire budget and we've already spent quite a bit, so how can we afford the plumbing?" another student asked.

We agreed that the water and drain lines were essential, but we began branching out to get alternative plans. And by the time we got to the fourth plumbing company, a small, local outfit led by a stereotypically gruff, burly plumber, an alternative presented itself.

"Welp," he said, "suppose you could just go through up there." He was pointing to the ceiling space above the proposed location.

"Up there?" I asked.

"Yep," he said. "Just go through the ceiling. Drop it down on the other side of the hallway and tie it in."

"Would it work?"

"Suppose so," he said, in a nonchalant manner intended to convey confidence. Strangely, it did.

"Would it be up to code?" I asked. Everything, I had discovered, had a "code" that "it had to be up to" and it was up to me to determine that everything, in fact, was up to it.

"I wouldn't do it if it weren't," he said.

"How much would that cost?" I asked.

"Prolly around $4,000."

"That's it?" I asked. "Four thousand for the whole job?"

He nodded in response.

"Sold," I said, smiling and turning to the team of students. We were off to the races and would officially have a sink. Or at least, the promise of one. The finished system was to include a sump pump placed in the corner of the bar area with several drain lines running to it—one from the sink, one from the espresso machine, and one from the glass rinser. A single line snaked from the pump straight up the wall, through the ceiling, and into the custodian closet twenty-five feet away.

Despite the plumbing being one of the first services we acquired, it ended up being one of the last to complete. With our deadline of September 1 looming, I found myself checking in every other day with the company to find out when they would be finishing. In the final stretch, the lead plumber himself came out to the school and set up a ladder in the hallway to finish running the drain line. A grouchy man by nature, he was especially perturbed to have students passing his ladder in the hall as they hurried by to get their class schedule for the upcoming year. Finally, in exasperation, he turned to one hurried freshman student, brand-new to the school, with the classic "deer in the headlights" look and let loose his rage.

"Do you want this or not?" he shouted.

The girl instantly froze and looked up at the overweight man, sweating profusely and leaning precariously on the ladder yelling in her direction.

"Well? Do you? 'Cause if you want this coffee thing or whatever, then you better let me finish my work!"

As the young woman hurried on her way, obviously terrified, he continued under his breath and proceeded to mutter a string of expletives before announcing, to all within earshot, that his high school never had a coffee bar, and he didn't understand why these students should be privy to one.

And just like that, we encountered our first sincere experience with generational jealousy toward the experiences we were providing our students. It's easy now, years later, to forget that it's not at all normal to have a full-service coffee bar perched just inside the entrance doors to a high school. But then, nothing that we would do over the coming years would be considered "normal" for a high school. Often, in conversation with parents who lament the fact that programming like this did not exist during their high school days, I reflect on the initial team of students who, years ago, with limited funds and a whole heap of persistence, helped usher a dream into reality over the course of a few months. Imagine the learning these students received—from navigating health department requirements and electric code to drawing a blueprint and planning equipment location—and how much value it added to their lives.

Another added intangible but valuable benefit the students gleaned was a sense of ownership. Contrary to the mobile coffee cart, this now-permanent coffee bar, still dubbed The Leaning Eagle, conveyed a clear accomplishment for these students. They felt the pride that only one who has suffered in the trench prior to victory can feel. They lived out the attributes that we wouldn't quantify and name for years to come: growth mindset, grit, redefining failure, and opportunity seeking. And in September of that school year, they got to see everything fall into place.

Every dollar in our budget was spent leading up to the grand opening. Along the way, we talked the school's business office into issuing us an official credit card so that we could make the necessary purchases without having to go through the hassle of a purchase order and payment request. The other thing the credit card enabled us to do, in a risky move that fortunately paid off, was to purchase additional necessary items in the weeks leading up to the grand opening and well after we had exhausted our funds. Banking on the belief that our grand opening would bring in a healthy dose of sales, we racked up an extensive credit card bill knowing that it would not need to be paid off until the third week of school. And in the days leading up to the grand opening, we hurried to finish all the necessary components.

They say that if you, as an entrepreneur, don't look back on your first product with a sense of embarrassment, then you waited too long to go to market. Such is true when you build a coffee bar—we learned more by what we didn't know at the time. Yes, mistakes were made. Yes, things were done out of order. Yes, it could have gone smoother. But, at the same time, it was perfect. The completed bar, during its grand opening, drew the attention not only of the 450 high school students, but of their parents, their teachers, and even several local news stations. And other schools took notice as well—that year we had more interest from local schools, both private and public, than any other year leading up to it.

All because we had a team of students managing a business on display for all to see.

And manage, they did. The coffee bar opened with an intentionally small menu and an impeccably trained crew. During the final weeks of construction, we partnered with a local roastery that came and provided official barista training for the students. One by one, these students mastered milk steaming, espresso shot pulling, brewing airpots of coffee, assembling drinks. They even dabbled in latte art, and several went on to become proficient in the skill.

By the end of the first week, we had not only far surpassed our sales goals, but had amassed a list of well over forty additional students who wanted to get involved.

"When I gave you permission to dream big," Dean said, surveying the bustling line and sense of excitement surrounding the bar at the grand opening, "I must admit, I did not anticipate this. Well done."

While the early success of the coffee bar was due largely to its newness and originality, the continued success was due to a recently established scheduling change at the school's policy level. In the early days of the mobile cart, Dean had helped the school transition from its archaic study hall model (think of the classic note passing, spitball shooting, forced silence kind of deal) into what was called personal responsibility time or PRT. The PRT model had grown out of the awareness that as our students matriculated to college, they often felt unprepared for the sudden burst of freedom their scheduling provided. After hearing from a few too many parents about how their students experienced a form of failure in the first semester due to this freedom, Dean and his administrative team began a course of investigation that led, after seeing the successful implementation at other schools, to this policy.

During PRT, students in grades nine through twelve have the freedom to move about campus unimpeded by hall passes or questioning teachers. Whether they congregate in the "theater commons" whiling their time away at ping-pong, or whether they shoot basketballs in the gym, work on papers in the library, or simply sit in a corner and chat with friends, they now had the freedom to decide how their time was spent. There was, as to be expected, an initial outcry from the parents of freshmen who saw the effect this freedom had on their children and protested that they needed more structure. Dean held firm and demonstrated that it was better to learn these lessons in the safety of a small high school campus than in the large, sprawling layout of a college. Not to mention that freshman year of college was significantly more expensive than freshman year of high school.

Slowly but surely, the parents came around and before long, the policy became deeply ingrained in our school culture. And its existence is directly tied to the continued success of The Leaning Eagle. When the bar was designed, the students were adamant that it contain bar top-style seating and be a place for students to hang out. As a result, The Leaning Eagle quickly became the hotspot for students during their PRT. And as any Starbucks can attest, the more people "hanging out," the more drinks end up getting sold.

The team of students assembled to transform the cart into the bar stayed a close-knit group for the duration of the year, helped along by the fact that all of them were current seniors. The fact of them being seniors had its clear advantages (leaders in the school, drivers of products, social clout), but it also had its soon-to-be-discovered disadvantages (all would graduate at the end of the year with no other managers left behind). Nonetheless, it was all part of the learning experience, both for the students and for me.

At the start of the year, we set a goal to double the gross revenue from the mobile coffee cart, which meant achieving $6,000 in sales. At the time, this seemed grandiose. In hindsight, it was incredibly short-sighted. One of the first rules with any goal-setting formula is to be sure the goal is big enough, and ours was simply not. This became apparent a few days after our grand opening when the school hosted the annual Meet the Teacher Night. During this event, parents are welcomed to an assembly where they get to go around and mimic their children's schedule while listening to a ten-minute pitch from each teacher. The event is highly attended and always brings with it a contagious energy for the school year ahead.

"We should open for Meet the Teacher Night," one of the students suggested during a meeting. "We'd get a lot of sales."

"True," another added. "We'd sell a ton of drinks."

"What if," I began, "we sold more than drinks. What if we sold gift certificates."

"Even better," another student said, "gift cards. Physical cards. I know we can, because I saw them online when we picked Square."

We had decided to use Square Services as a point-of-sale system as this made for easy collection of sales data and daily deposits in a school-owned bank account. And when the coffee bar opened, roughly 40 percent of sales were with credit cards. After looking over the Square website, it became clear that physical plastic gift cards would work and we decided to rush an order for the event. This required making a decision about a logo. Rather than take months to meet with the visual art department and commission a student-created logo design, we opted for a $15 service that generated a logo within minutes. The finished product looked sharp and we slapped it on the gift cards that arrived two days prior to the event.

I assembled the team the night of the event and gave what I can only imagine was a Braveheart-inspired speech about the importance of seizing this opportunity to showcase the bar to parents and jump-start our sales for the year. We would strive for $500 in total gift card sales as that would get us one-twelfth of the way to our overall goal for the year. The students looked on and nodded in agreement, faces solemn as they considered the task ahead of them. This was their moment—everything had led up to this and now it was game time.

Nothing, however, could have prepared us for what happened next.

Earlier that day, we had shared our plans with Dean to sell gift cards during the event. We even went so far as to explain, in a moment of brilliance, that we would hand deliver the cards the following day to each student. Dean, unbeknownst to us, took this directive to heart. That night, as parents were taking their seats in the standing-room-only five-hundred-seat auditorium, Dr. Dean Nicholas, the principal of the school, proceeded to list all the amazing opportunities that awaited their students this school year.

"And," he said, beginning to wrap up before dismissing them to hear from the teachers, "I am excited to share that you will be witness to the grand opening of our brand-new permanent coffee bar, The Leaning Eagle."

There was a smattering of applause.

"Also," he said, a devious smile forming, "they are selling gift cards tonight that will be hand-delivered to students tomorrow. And I would hate, I would absolutely be distraught if your student was the only one not to get one."

And with that, our destiny was sealed.

The line that formed was instantaneous and lasted for the duration of the three-hour evening. Gift cards were being signed right and left, and brewed coffee became a fast-flowing river as the students struggled just to keep up with demand. Wholly unprepared for this, we had to quickly assemble four boxes for the gift cards just to separate the grades. In an effort to ensure that their students were covered, we had dozens of people buying gift cards for their students unaware that their spouse had just purchased one as well.

I was caught, torn between the sessions I was conducting with my sophomore English class, and running back out to the coffee bar to survey the madness. I had the Square sales report pulled up on my phone and was refreshing the screen every thirty seconds, even during my talk. I'm sure parents that night felt their students were in class with a distracted madman, but perhaps they too were only worried about getting out of the session so they could get in line for a The Leaning Eagle gift card.

At the evening's conclusion, a team of students, exhausted but exhilarated, gathered around the bar surveying the imposing stack of gift cards.

"Well," asked one of the students, addressing the group. "What was our total?"

I hit the refresh button on the screen.

"It's a bit more than $500," I said, covering the screen with my hand.

"How much more, like $1,000?" a student asked.

"I bet it's more like $2,000," another said.

"We ended the night with a grand total of $4,950," I said, a massive smile spreading over my face.

"The night's not over yet," said a voice behind me.

We all turned and saw Dean standing there holding his credit card out with a beckoning flick of his wrist.

"I'd like a $50 gift card," he said.

There are stories from our high school experience that, like the immortal mythologies of the Greeks, live on in retelling throughout our lives. Whether it is a prom night fiasco or a winning touchdown in the final minutes of a game, these stories weave themselves into our lives like a colorful fabric whose tapestry informs our autobiography.

Those students, standing there that evening in the middle of Miracle Commons, facing the coffee bar they had created, had just witnessed such an experience. For the rest of their lives, they will tell the story of the night they sold $5,000 worth of gift cards. But more than that, they will tell of dreams and goals, of ambitions and success. They will lean back and say that hard work and determination pay off and that it's better to put yourself out and there and try than to choose the safe, secure route.

They will also tell you that it's a lot easier to pay off a $10,000 loan when you make $5,000 in a single day.

CHAPTER THREE

"Serving as a manager at the coffee bar taught me a lot of skills that can't be learned from a textbook. Concepts like customer service, marketing, and PR all need practice, and at the coffee bar, I could get a little better each day at each of those. I was able to apply those skills (directly and indirectly) to clubs and internships in college as well as my job now."

— Jeremy, '16

The Leaning Eagle Coffee Bar was a resounding success. Beginning with its launch in a permanent location in the fall of 2016, the concept more than proved the hypothesis that a group of high school students would want to (and be able to) run a business. The unexpected side effect, however, became the number of students seeking involvement. The nature of the coffee bar and its size and design allowed for a maximum of two or three students working as a group at any one time. And the nature of our school day allowed for nine of these groups.

It's worth explaining the format we established for this as it differs from student ventures at other schools. First, our students are enrolled in a class that appears on their schedule as "Entrepreneurship Internship." This class means that during that particular bell, the student's "classroom" is actually the coffee bar.

Rather than have the coffee bar open just in the morning before school, or just after school, our desire was to have it open all day long, from 7:30 a.m. until 3:30 p.m., in order to guarantee coffee service any time school was in session. Part of this philosophy stemmed from the reasoning behind the business in the first place.

Much like any solid entrepreneurial exercise, the coffee cart had originated not only out of a desire to let students run a business but also to solve a clear and specific problem—student tardies. It is a well-known fact that first bell classes will have to suffer the frustration and productivity loss from regular tardies, but what made matters worse was the fact that these perpetually late students would arrive balancing a Starbucks cup along with their books. When the attempt to crack down on the tardies failed and a ban on Starbucks was not even considered (out of fear of teacher mutiny), the notion of an in-house solution presented itself.

When a student shows up for class at their "Entrepreneurship Internship," they don an apron, wash their hands, and get to work managing the coffee bar. During the bell they will make a variety of drinks, restock supplies, clean the counters, and chat with the people hanging out during PRT. It is about as far away from the traditional classroom atmosphere as possible. And we wanted it this way. It also means that these groups of students are largely self-monitored. This is where the placement of the coffee bar became one of its biggest assets. Because it was located just inside the main doors of the high school, it is situated just feet from the front office desk where it can be monitored by two administrative leads. In addition to the added benefit of always having adult eyes on the students working the bar, this also gave me a way to be present without being present. If anything went awry, I would be notified immediately. If anyone did not show up for their bell, it was recorded. If a particular music playlist ventured into the borderline obscene, I would be able to address it.

In other words, I had spies.

This concept carried over into our next system of routine checks. In the establishment of the coffee bar, the students who were part of the design and implementation team each took one of the bells to oversee. In that bell, we placed one or two additional students who would form their "mini-team." This created a hierarchal structure to the coffee bar, which helped with the dissemination of new information and planning. The managing students (bell leaders) met with me once a week to go over sales, inventory, and future planning, and then they would each communicate this with their bells.

It was during one of these meetings that the topic of secret shoppers came up.

"What do you think?" I asked. "Would you be open to the idea?"

"How would it work?" they asked.

"Basically, I would select a few random people, students and adults alike, and have them come to the bar unannounced, order a drink, review the experience, and report back to me."

"Kind of like a quality control check," one student said. "We do that at my job."

"Exactly," I said. "All in favor?"

The secret shopper program took off in exciting ways—at all times the students were ready, expecting each and every customer to be the one evaluating them. Often, they would look slyly up after making the drink, and ask, "So, will it be a good review?" And just as often they were met with a confused look. The feedback from the secret shoppers enabled me to be even more present with the bar. The first year, my biggest difficulty was balancing my full-time teaching load with the management of the bar. On an eight-bell schedule, I was teaching five classes and using one bell for lunch, which left two bells where I could consistently be at the bar. This led to a flurry of creative approaches on my end—whether it was a short in-class assignment I gave my students so I could sneak out and see how the students were doing at the bar, or whether I commissioned one of my own students to be a secret shopper on the spot and asked them to give a full report upon returning to the room.

The biggest thing I remember from that first year, apart from the excitement of the new bar, was the chaotic attempt to do everything. I was still operating under the notion that I could manage everything myself and that to admit anything to the contrary was a sign of weakness. I was still coaching cross country, still leading the debate club, teaching a full load, and managing a thriving business. Add this to the fact that I had a five-year-old daughter and a newborn son at home and a wife who had just started back to work full-time.

Something had to give. And quick.

I started with cross country—and the decision was not made lightly. Three years prior, I was overjoyed to take the leadership role in coaching the team and grow it into a respectable program. Running brings me one of my primary joys in life and the cross-country team enabled me to share this love with a core group of committed students. But I also knew that I could no longer continue to keep up the schedule I was keeping. After I sat down to do some serious cost-benefit analysis, I discovered that, although I enjoyed the coaching, the amount of extra money it was bringing in did not supersede the amount of time necessary for the commitment. I informed the team in a somber meeting that I would not be returning the next year and explained my reason as wanting more balance in my life so I could engage more with my own family.

And I have never once regretted it.

That began a mission for me where I began to evaluate all new experiences through the lens of a cost-benefit analysis. Would this new activity add value to my life that would exceed the amount of time it will require to complete? If the answer is no, then I try my hardest to say no to it. As ridiculous as this may sound, it was incredibly hard. Saying no, for me, went against every fiber of my being. Saying no was to say "I can't," which is a defeatist mindset.

Except that it isn't. The lesson I learned was not only that I cannot do everything but that it is OK to say no. In fact, it is more than OK—it is necessary. It may be too much to get our administrators to stop asking teachers to do everything and anything under the sun, but it is certainly in the realm of possibility to get our teachers to start saying no when they need to say no. Our time is a finite resource and is far more valuable than money—every time we say "yes" to something, we are saying "no" to something else and we must take all of that into consideration before accepting a new responsibility.

New responsibilities always come with new challenges. The coffee bar, for all of its excitement and joy and energizing spirit, brought with it a litany of unexpected challenges. One of these challenges was assessments.

"So how will you be grading them?" Sarah asked, looking over my course description. Sarah represented the counseling office at the school and the guru for all things related to grading and transcripts.

"Participation mostly," I said. "I was thinking ten points a week for doing what they are supposed to do."

"And that works," Sarah said, "but I was mostly referring to the grade on the transcript. Will this be a pass/fail course or a letter grade?"

"Probably pass/fail," I said. "That just sounds easier."

"And it is easier," she said, with hesitation, "but not necessarily better. It's about how seriously you want them to take the class. If you do a pass/fail, less work for you, but in the end, they won't prioritize the class as much and you won't be able to really reward the hard workers."

"So, a letter grade," I said. "I can make that work, but I'm going to need to figure out a way to get more grades."

Sarah smiled and nodded.

All that sounded well and good, but how was I going to get more grades if the class met at the coffee bar and didn't have a teacher? On a regular basis, I was only physically present with about 20 percent of the students and the remaining 80 percent were on their own with me relying on secret shoppers and observations from the office staff. Additionally, I was hesitant to assign outside work as the students were already overburdened with homework, athletic practice, extracurriculars, and more. And yet, every day they came to the coffee bar to work, they *were* learning. The learning was as real and practical as anything else and we had to figure out a way to quantify it. I started by likening it to *The Karate Kid.*

"Each day you all are waxing on and waxing off. You're painting the house and sanding the deck. Each day you're making lattes, cleaning and restocking, providing customer service. And it feels like work, day in and day out. But in the end, look at what you've learned—resilience, initiative, work ethic, and problem-solving."

They were living out everything we had talked about regarding innovative education. They had truly moved beyond the walls of the traditional classroom and into something quite possibly even more important.

But how to grade that.

By the end of the semester, I had a plan. Project-based learning models had been around for a while, and this class was primed for such an assessment. The idea was to have the students, while they were managing and operating the coffee bar, begin the process of pitching a new business idea. During the ideation stage, which they could do with their team or even with customers at the coffee bar, they would brainstorm problems faced by the students at the school on a regular basis. Based off these problems, they would start to propose a variety of solutions that could turn into potential business ideas for implementation at the school. I intentionally limited it to businesses at the school in the hope that we would get an idea that could provide additional spots for students on our waiting list. During the customer research stage, they went out and conducted interviews, finding students from all grade levels, and determining if their proposed solution would be met with success. They would then move into market research, financials, and goals before putting together a compelling business plan.

I was able to grade each component of these plans as it was due and use this as a secondary grade category for the class. The students would receive a ten-point weekly grade on participation (based on attendance, secret shopper reports, and my own interactions) and they would also receive regular grades based on pieces of their plan. In the gradebook, the categories were divided evenly so that the project-based component awarded 50 percent of the letter grade. This also ensured that I would have a letter grade for each student at the end of the quarter as well as semester.

"This business plan," I announced to the team, "will be presented at a special evening event in April."

"Will there be food?" asked one of the students.

"Yes," I said, smiling, "there will be food. But you have to dress up when you pitch your business."

"That's fine," the student said, "as long as there's food."

After putting together a series of due dates and guidelines, the students were off, managing a new business while dreaming up ideas for future ones. As the April event loomed nearer, the students put the finishing touches on multipage plans and began to workshop their pitches. The evening event went over as smoothly as possible. I had made the decision to not invite parents this year as I wasn't quite sure what would happen, but in hindsight, I should have invited the entire school. The students were proud of their ideas and the work put into them and the energy in the room was strong. One by one, they got up, explained the problem they were trying to solve, walked through their business plan, and, in *Shark Tank* style, asked for the necessary funding to start the business. Most of the ideas were what you would expect, ranging from pop-up school stores featuring writing utensils and charging cables to school spirit wear design shops. One student pitched "The Scoop," which was a mobile ice cream unit, and another proposed a bakery.

It was the last presentation, however, where I thought we finally hit on the next idea. Sam got up to describe his problem and hit us with a slew of convincing data. He demonstrated how an incredible percentage of high school students come to school without breakfast. His proposed "breakfast bar" included a blueprint and layout using existing space in our theater commons and seemed to be a viable solution to the problem he had just outlined. As he went through each detail, I began to visualize the space more and more. He ended by describing the student experience at what he termed "Blend":

"They walk in, hurried because they are running late, and they realize they forgot to eat breakfast."

Sam mimicked the panicking, late-running student in pantomime.

"But no worries—they swing by Blend and grab a healthy smoothie and some granola and just like that, they are off to a great day."

Just like that. This was it. Fresh off the success of the coffee bar in its inaugural year as a permanent fixture in the school, I had gotten it in my mind that we would need to open a new business each year to keep up with the growing student demand. And this concept, this breakfast bar idea, would be perfect for the following year. My excitement was due to several components:

First, this would play right into my passion for healthy eating as it would help students choose healthier options for breakfast. Second, the space, proposed in the high school concessions stand, was already in existence and would require far less work to become operational.

"Thank you, everyone," I said at the conclusion of the evening. "Phenomenal work and a solid year."

The students fell into celebration not only for the completion of their semester-long project, but also for the stellar performance of The Leaning Eagle Coffee Bar, which brought in over $25,000 in gross revenue. Things could not have gone better and for this reason, I made the decision, then and there, that our next venture would be "Blend"—a smoothie breakfast bar that would blow the coffee bar out of the water and be an even larger success.

CHAPTER FOUR

"I learned that when something doesn't work out the way you thought it would, it wasn't a failure. It often laid the groundwork for the next idea that launched me into something beyond what I could've imagined the first time around. I learned to redefine what failure meant and to push toward success."

— Mollie, '22

I'll cut to the chase—Blend was a failure. The smoothie bar was doomed from the start. The writing was on the wall, but I was too caught up in the momentum of success to interpret it. I include its story here because, as you'll see throughout this book, the notion of embracing failure is central to the entrepreneurial mindset. When I say that the smoothie bar was a failure, I don't look at that as a bad thing—if anything, it was one of the most important learnings in the history of the entrepreneurship program and I wouldn't ever wish it didn't happen. Would I go back and change a whole litany of things? Of course, but that's the beauty of hindsight and of learning from mistakes. The entrepreneurship program would not be where it is today if we hadn't taken the risk of exploring a second start-up concept.

The first mistake I made was assembling a group of students and asking them to carry out the vision cast by a now-graduated senior. They were handed the business plan and charged with implementing it. Of course it's easy to see why this was problematic: Not only was it not their vision but it did not connect fully to their *why*. Someone else's dream had been placed squarely in their lap and they were asked to make it come true. We learned, firsthand, that without adequate buy-in from the team, the dream will wither. For the entire first semester, the leadership team lolled around, idly tossing ideas back and forth but never taking action. I prodded and suggested and cajoled, but nothing happened. They would go through bursts of excitement but when it came time to take action on any key step, they would falter.

Part of the problem stemmed from my inability to spend enough quality time with them in the planning phase. Even after dropping cross country, my schedule had remained packed, and with a full teaching load plus oversight of The Leaning Eagle Coffee Bar, I was pulled in too many directions to play a meaningful role. These days, when I speak to schools about the three components necessary for a successful director of entrepreneurship, I focus on freedom, autonomy, and resources. I'm always quick to then add "but not too much" with all three of these points. The "not too much" learning stemmed largely from this smoothie bar experience—I gave the project over entirely to the students and asked them to fulfill it, gave them a budget, and left them alone. Their overall inaction suggested that they needed more teacher intervention.

Intervene I did—too much and too fast. In desperation to avoid the project being labeled a "failure," I swooped in and attempted to save face. First, I talked my wife into giving up a few days of Christmas break to help repaint the concessions space. We paid a babysitter and then, instead of heading to a nice restaurant or movie, we came to the school, laid out a drop cloth, and began to paint. Then, our illustrious art teacher designed, printed, and installed a sign for the space, prominently displaying "Blend" as a space for healthy smoothies and breakfast bites. I then purchased several blenders, came up with some specialty toast recipes to start off the menu, and proceeded to create an onboarding manual for the students when they returned.

At the end of Christmas break, I presented Blend, our hastily constructed smoothie breakfast bar, to the group of six students tasked with the project. You can see, I imagine, the immediate problem up front—everything was me. I had orchestrated all this work and had not pulled in the student team whatsoever. Tempers flared.

"So, wait," one of the student leaders said, "you just did this all without us over Christmas break?"

"Yeah, Mr. Carter," another said, "we would have been glad to help. This is what we signed up for, after all. You didn't even ask."

"The fact is," I said, "the whole first semester is gone, and I wanted you to have a business to run. Well, now you have a business."

The grumbling I got in return was much different than the excitement from the student leaders the previous year over The Leaning Eagle. I worked to save face as much as possible and got everyone excited about a grand opening in a few weeks. Fortunately, they were able to exercise creative control over the smoothie recipes in a way that gave them enough of a sense of ownership to give them motivation to move along. Over the next two weeks, they settled on a premade smoothie mix (Dr. Smoothie) and conducted training with about twenty underclassmen students to fully staff the bar during the school day. The plan was to open forty-five minutes before the start of school and to continue operations throughout the day, transitioning from specialty toast to lunch sandwiches to after-school snacks with smoothies all along the way. There was even a protein smoothie for the student athletes.

Enough excitement was generated during this planning period to ensure a successful launch and the opening day did make quite the splash. The students brought in well over $500 in gross sales and had a fantastic time doing so. And this honeymoon period continued for the first week. By the second week, sales had dropped to about $250 a day, and by the third week, it was down to $100. It didn't help that also during the third week, a massive fountain constructed by the physics students was erected in the middle of our theater commons, completely blocking the entrance and visibility of the new business.

"Things will improve when the fountain gets removed in a month," I told the students.

A month passed, and things did not improve. By this point, the business was bringing in about $50 a day. It was at this point that we encountered our second obstacle—the cafeteria program. Without belaboring the point, suffice to say, our cafeteria, operated by a third-party vendor, was not happy having competition from a group of students just down the hall. They pointed to a "noncompete" clause in their contract that caused us to have to shut down operations for 30 percent of the school day. While this made for some interesting discussions with the student leadership team, it ultimately damaged the morale of the students and further tanked sales. At this point, we were desperate—we ditched the healthy image and tried afternoon milkshakes, morning cinnamon rolls, and we even launched a "true Belgian waffle" product line that involved a two-rise and bake process, which meant we had to have a delegate (usually me) show up around 5 a.m. to start the dough. All this work, all this ideation and creation and effort, and still no success.

The smoothie breakfast bar continued to languish for the remainder of the year, and by the end of the year, though I was willing to throw in the towel, I was given enough encouragement from the student leadership team to try it again the following year. I staffed the bar carefully and implemented a strict protocol of training and did everything I knew to do (even going so far as to have a camera system installed so I could monitor the business from my classroom). Still, it was clear early on, this was not a business destined for greatness.

"What made the difference?" I asked myself many times in frustration. "The coffee bar took off and this business died a slow, miserable death."

In the end, there seemed to be a few key components that led to the failure of the venture (other than the lack of overall student buy-in). First was its location. While the coffee bar is in a central spot in the school that every single student passes multiple times a day, the smoothie bar was placed at the far end of our building where only the most dedicated (and hungry) of students would pass by. Someone had to go out of their way to get a smoothie. It was placed here thinking it would capture students on their way in during the morning, but this led to another realization:

students who arrived having skipped breakfast were in such a hurry to get to class that they didn't even have time to swing by the smoothie bar.

In other words, the best-laid plans (in this case by stellar coffee bar managers) don't always work out. And survey feedback is not always the most reliable when determining a course of action. Having taken all this into consideration, I called an emergency meeting of all Blend managers and shared the sad news that we would be shutting our doors a full twelve months after we opened.

"Effective when?" Jake asked. Jake, Dean Nicholas's son, was currently a sophomore and in his first year in the program. He was also the exact opposite of traditional student. Because of my role, I worked with Jake both in the entrepreneurship environment as well as the English classroom and saw two drastically different sides of him. The care and attention to detail he put into his work with running a business was diametrically opposed to the lack of passion he had for any assigned classroom work. Jake could not be bothered to spend an hour writing a paper on a work of literature, but he had no problem spending days obsessing over a business venture. And as a result, he is exactly the kind of student who thrives in this nontraditional programming.

"Immediately," I said, seeing Jake's spirit begin to crumble. "Today's our last day."

"What are we supposed to do?" asked another student.

"Those of you enrolled in the class will continue to work on entrepreneurship materials and those of you who are volunteering your time can go on to other things."

"Mr. Carter," Jake said, "what about the coffee bar?"

"The coffee bar is fine and doing well," I said. "It will not be closing."

"No," he said, "what if the smoothie bar moves to the coffee bar. Like what if we merge the two?"

"We wouldn't be able to," I said, too quickly. "We don't have enough electric set up to run the blenders and our space is limited. Plus, there's no equipment for the food or anything."

What I didn't say was that I had no desire to merge the two—Blend had been nothing but a hassle and I wanted it to be done.

"Seems like it would be possible," said Jake, with an air of persistence. "Besides, aren't we supposed to be learning how we should try different ideas to solve problems."

Now he had me in a tight place—he was right, of course, but my concern ran deeper. I feared if we merged the businesses, the bad vibes from the smoothie bar would trickle into the coffee bar and we would breed more failure. What I was experiencing, in other words, was fear. And that fear was preventing me from acting. Fortunately, Jake was having none of it.

"Could we at least try?" he asked.

Try—could we at least try? What a question. And a question that Jake shouldn't have to ask. Of course we *can* try; in fact, we *must* try. Trying is what those with an entrepreneurial mindset do, trying is how we learn, trying is how we grow. Now, years later, I look back on this conversation and smile. Here we were, or really, here *I* was, mired in failure, and ready to give up. Yet, here was this student, this nontraditional, classroom-despising student who was embodying the entrepreneurial mindset in a real, visceral way and encouraging us to see things from a different perspective. He was the one with the necessary mindset.

"I tell you what," I said. "If you think it will work, I want you to do it. I want you to oversee the transition and make it successful—I believe you are the best person for the job."

And with that, Jake took charge of merging the two businesses. The Leaning Eagle effectively subsumed Blend—the blenders were moved down, and a portion of the coffee bar was turned into a smoothie area. The food items were scrapped altogether, and the smoothies were reinvented using real, organic fruit instead of premade smoothie mix. Within a month of the merger, the gross sales at the coffee bar had doubled. What had been deemed a failure was now a success packaged in a valuable learning lesson. It's OK, we learned, to fail. It's OK to try new things. It's OK to branch out into the unknown, to test the market, to ideate and create and explore. And it's OK to trip and fall and bruise up your ego. Because, as we discovered and would continue to discover year after year after year, true failure would have been if we had not tried in the first place.

CHAPTER FIVE

"The entrepreneurship program gave me a real-life look into running a small business, including the fun and creative side of it that comes with not having a boss, but also the tough side of it that comes with being the boss. It also solidified my decision to pursue an entrepreneurial career because no matter what new challenge popped up on that week's to-do list, I was always excited to take it on and combine business knowledge and sales numbers with the creative side of things."

— Alana, '17

As things continued to take off for the burgeoning entrepreneurship program (including a snack stand in the seventh-to-eighth-grade building and a wait list for students wanting to manage The Leaning Eagle), I continued to teach English mostly full-time. I say "mostly" because of my six bells; two were dedicated to overseeing entrepreneurship and four were dedicated to English. Of these English bells, I had three sections of a sophomore honors class that was my pride and joy. This was the course that I had poured so much of myself into teaching and had, over the years, developed into something I was intensely proud of. One of the most discussed features of this class was the food unit. This unit had drawn enough attention among the students at the school that most incoming sophomores had preconceived notions about what to expect. The unit served multiple purposes at once: First, it drew in high-level nonfiction reading content that introduced students to Lexile reading scores far above high school level. Second, it allowed me to get into the weeds with a personal passion of mine—local food. Finally, it made students think.

Each year the food unit would grow in length. What had started as a two-week experiment grew into a full-quarter (nine weeks) length complete with multiple books and articles, two documentaries, a series of classroom debates, and a final presentation of original research. And each year there would be a contingent of students who wanted to go deeper.

"Mr. Carter," they would ask, "what's next? Can we visit a local farm or maybe start a garden?"

I would smile and tell them they were welcome to set it up and I was happy to support their efforts. Usually, this amounted to nothing. Until, that is, the day that Julie started asking. Julie is one of those students that teachers either love or hate—her infectious curiosity for learning is only suited to educators who still care about their craft. And her type of student can detect that in a teacher within minutes.

"So, Mr. Carter," she said, smiling, "you're telling me that you're comfortable just introducing us to these important concepts and then letting us go about our lives as normal? You're not wanting us to reach for systematic change or legislation?"

"Well, Julie," I said, "I'll tell you the same thing I tell the other students who ask for additional class time devoted to the food unit—you go out and set up an interesting experience or opportunity, and then we can talk."

"I respect that, Mr. Carter," she said, "but I've been talking to a few other teachers about this, and I have an idea that I think you should pursue."

"I'm listening," I said, already planning my refusal. I had been working on saying no more often.

"We've been reading great articles by a few authors and unlike the other books we read in this class, these authors are still alive. Like they're still *alive*! Breathing and all."

"True," I said, intrigued.

"So," she said, "you should get a few of them to come speak. Here. To us. Bring them to our campus."

Bring them to our campus. Wow. OK, I thought, now that would be pretty cool.

"What would that look like?" I pushed back.

"I don't know," she said, "but we're always having these discussions and debates in class and maybe we should bring in the authors and confront them with our arguments. I think it would be cool."

"It would," I said, starting to get genuinely excited. "It really would."

"Maybe," she said, "you can even get that crazy farmer guy you showed us on YouTube—the one who was in *Food, INC*."

"Joel Salatin," I said, the idea now coming to fruition in my mind. "Yes, Joel Salatin here at Cincinnati Hills Christian Academy—wouldn't that be something."

"Just an idea, Mr. Carter. Thanks!"

And with that, Julie was gone, but what she had planted in my mind began to grow and take off and develop and turned into something so much larger than any of us could have anticipated. In retrospect, much of the program's success is due to student engagement. And not just engaging students, but chasing this engagement when the opportunity presented itself. Here was a high-school sophomore student legitimately interested in learning more about food systems and sustainability and in that moment the bigger problem seemed to be what would happen if we *didn't* chase it down. After all, when students come alive in the educational process, it becomes a validation for the act itself. And so, the next step of the journey was made manifest.

One of the consistent motifs present in this story is an ongoing mission to ask for a certain amount of money from the school and getting, in return, only a small fraction of the ask. Although this is always frustrating in the moment, I've come to see it as one of the key aspects of the program's ongoing success. The Food Symposium, as this idea came to be called, is one such example.

In the few years since the inception of the entrepreneurship program, the school, under the direction of then head Randy Brunk, had developed a teacher innovation grant fund. As part of a capital campaign called "Light the Way" (which also helped provide the funds to build our four-thousand-square-foot greenhouse that will play a pivotal role in the story of the program), it was decided that to help teachers pursue innovative ideas both in and out of the classroom, funding should be in place. Throughout the campaign, a portion of the funds were directed to this account until the account held over $1 million. At this point, it was introduced to the teachers.

The concept was extraordinary—if a teacher had an idea for something different and innovative that would engage students, they could apply for a grant not from some faceless governmental organization but from the school itself. If the idea got approved, the teacher didn't have to wait for a year to get the funding—they got it right away. The only flaw in the system, from a teacher's perspective, was the massive hoop that had to be jumped through via the online grant proposal process. Modeled after a traditional grant-seeking process, a teacher had to provide financials, a clear breakdown, myriad resources, and more original research just to be considered. Then the idea went to a committee and the process could take months to get going. This tedious process stymied more than one innovative idea and kept several teachers from even attempting to get the funding.

Perhaps it's the English teacher in me, but I tend to not shy away from mountains of paperwork if it means working toward a clear goal. And the visualization of having Joel Salatin visit our campus to talk to our students was enough to motivate me to complete the multipage process. My ask was clear: $25,000 to facilitate and run a small-scale conference that would include a keynote speaker, food trucks, breakout sessions, and more. I even thought it would be neat to have a few vendors set up tables for the event. I tackled the grant and went through the process and waited for the committee feedback. When several months rolled by and I still heard nothing, I continued in my persistence. Finally I was notified, via email, that I had been awarded a grant. The amount, far less than my ask, came in at $10,000.

I was simultaneously overjoyed and frustrated. Overjoyed that I now had some funds to accomplish this task but frustrated that the $10,000 would only cover Joel Salatin's speaking fee, leaving the rest of the event completely without funds. This is where, in hindsight, I see the beauty in the decision by the grant committee. By not giving me the full amount I asked for, I was being forced to either give up or develop the grit and creativity necessary to succeed. I was, in essence, being forced to embrace the entrepreneurial spirit. And I dove it headfirst.

The next nine months were a whirlwind of learning experiences, trials, failures, minor successes, triumphs, and exhaustion. For funding, I began a journey of understanding how to get sponsors. I traveled all over the city, introducing myself and sharing the vision, getting rejected time and time again until finally several organizations said yes. Then I made the decision to charge a ticket price to help cover costs. This meant promoting the event to drive sales, which led to a crash course on marketing and online promotion. In the midst of all this, the event grew from a small one-off speaking engagement to the full-scale CHCA Food Symposium: Pathway to Sustainability, spanning two days with two keynote speakers (Joel Salatin and Simran Sethi), thirty-five breakout speakers, and twenty-four sponsors. In the end, we had over five hundred paying attendees, and 65 percent of them had no prior affiliation with the school—they were coming for the speakers and the topic. The food truck rally was a massive success and we ended up with an expo hall in our gymnasium that featured over forty-five booths. Our admissions team worked around the clock giving tours and scheduled visits for prospective students.

It was the single hardest undertaking of my entire career—harder even than overseeing the build-out of the coffee bar. And yet it was also the most rewarding. At the center of it all, was this notion of the entrepreneurial mindset—of seeing an opportunity and seizing it for all it was worth. It also helped usher in a clarity around our message of entrepreneurship. Because we were focusing in on food system sustainability for the event, it made sense to work with the coffee bar on developing a greater sense of sustainability. During the buildup to the event, I worked closely with the current team of The Leaning Eagle managers to undergo a massive shift in ideology and mission. It became clear that if we were going to host an event around food sustainability that captured this idea of properly stewarding the earth, then we had to follow suit with our business and ensure we were doing everything possible to set an example. Our mission was clear and straightforward: lower our carbon footprint as much as possible.

This process took us on an exciting journey that started, of all places, at Whole Foods. Drawn to their clear mission and sense of purpose, I took a group of students to meet with the local store manager.

"It's about doing what's right," he said, standing in the back room surrounded by pallets and unboxed produce. "We believe in doing the right thing simply because it's the right thing to do."

"What about the cost?" one of my students asked.

"We decided early on," the manager continued, "that if we do it because it's right, then the customers who care about that will come to us. Start with what's right and you'll attract the right customer."

None of us had the terminology at the time, but we had just been given a crash course in defining a customer avatar. Our ideal customer at The Leaning Eagle was not just any person walking by but rather someone who cared about quality products that were sustainable. And this meant we had our work cut out for us.

We started with the products themselves—we worked with our local roasting company to better understand the topic of direct trade coffee and the way in which the coffee farmers and plantation owners are treated. We dove into ideas around living wages and packaging costs. We took tours of the roasting and packaging room and studied the process. Then we moved to the milk—after watching several distressing food documentaries in class (*Eating Animals* among the list), our team made the decision to closely examine where our milk was coming from, how the cows were treated, and what the cows were fed. The result was distressing to say the least. Our milk, purchased as cheaply as possible from the local grocery store, came to represent everything we were trying to raise awareness against. Thus began our campaign to find a local dairy farm—a campaign that ended in Wooster, Ohio, at a place called Hartzler Dairy.

Hartzler Dairy had us at hello—their website explained that their cows were grass-fed and allowed to rotate around the pasture. The milk was non-homogenized and low-temperature pasteurized. It was then delivered in glass bottles that were to be rinsed, sent back to the dairy, and reused. And to cap it off, the dairy delivered the milk every Thursday just two days after the milking and bottling process. We had found our product solution.

We then moved on to the packaging—while we weren't using Styrofoam for our drinks, we weren't exactly setting a standard either. I created a team solely to research compostable cups and this led to a rabbit hole around composting in general, which resulted in the awareness that while compostable cups did exist, they could not be composted in a general backyard system. This threw us for a loop as our original plan was to build a compost bin on campus to compost all the waste from the coffee bar. We went back to the drawing board and before too long, discovered our solution: GoZero. GoZero was a commercial compost program that sent carbon-neutral trucks, once or twice a month, to pick up compost (which was placed in neon bins by the dumpsters) and take it to a commercial facility where it would be turned back to soil and delivered to local farms.

Now came the hard part—the pricing. Up to this point, The Leaning Eagle had been operating with a 50 percent profit margin so for any $3 drink, we were netting $1.50 in profit. This was based on the cheaper milk and cheaper cups. Once we ran the numbers using the compostable products (cups, lids, sleeves, straws), grass-fed milk, and high-quality locally roasted coffee, the results were staggering—our $1.50 drink now cost over $3 just to make.

"We can't do this," one of our managers quipped. "It's too expensive and no one will buy it."

"Yeah," said another, "we'd have to charge $5 or more just to make a profit."

There were general murmurs of consent and feelings of frustration before one young lady stepped up.

"Remember Whole Foods," she said. "We do it because it's right. The customers will come."

Over the next half hour, the students debated back and forth before deciding that it was in the best interest of the coffee bar to move forward with the sustainability plan and raise prices across the board. We were coming up on the semester break, and they thought that seemed the best possible time to release the new prices, hoping students would forget the previous prices over the holiday break. To ease the overall burden on the coffee bar, it was also decided to cease offering the expensive reward program hosted through Square.

The reward program allows businesses to reward customers for their purchases through stars—every ten stars, one free drink. The advantage is the digital system—rather than mess with paper cards and stamps, this kept track of everything online. The disadvantage is the price—the service began at a rather low monthly fee before kicking up its pricing dependent on the number of customers the business serviced. In the end, we were paying over $125 a month for this service, and it didn't seem to bring a lot to the table. And so, The Leaning Eagle opened with its new higher pricing, new sustainable mission, and absent reward program in January of 2019.

And it flopped. Spectacularly.

First, all the students talked about was how expensive everything was. Then the pricing became fodder for a skit during the school's improv show. Then the reality about the reward system going away began to settle in. All at once, our sales tanked. And tanked. So, we were stuck with expensive (but sustainable) milk, lots of heart and purpose, and no sales. And no sales, of course, was problematic for a business.

"What do we do?" the students asked during our meetings. "Do we go back to the way things used to be? Do we change the prices? Serve the cheaper milk?"

It was decided that the best thing to do was to survey the customers. Through a series of methods, the students began collecting data regarding the recent changes at the coffee bar and they came to an interesting twofold discovery: The customers were woefully unaware of the new sustainability mission (and its impact on the prices) and the customers were furious about the lack of a rewards system. In other words, the pricing was the issue as much as the spread of knowledge and the feeling of betrayal at not rewarding regular customers.

Without knowing it, we had inadvertently stumbled upon the creation of a customer avatar. Through the hands-on, frantic process of trying to understand our dip in sales, the students had created an ideal customer profile, which had then given us a clear target for marketing our product. If we had sat around and imagined our ideal customer, we probably would have arrived at the conclusion that our ideal customer is a CHCA student. But instead, we determined that our ideal customer is someone who cares about quality and/or sustainably sourced products. Further, someone who has a generous mindset and appreciates our work to fund a scholarship program with our profits (that scholarship included regular deposits into a fund that could be accessed, via letter, by students who wanted to travel for our intercession experiences but could not afford it).

Thus began our marketing campaign. We devised a clear, concise mission statement for The Leaning Eagle that had three components—products, planet, profit. The finished statement read, "At The Leaning Eagle, we are dedicated to serving the highest quality, sustainably sourced products and to help fund a scholarship with our profits." I realize that any business or marketing book will dive deeply into the how behind the executive's role in the creation of the mission statement and its alignment with core values, but what we discovered as we were building this program, is that the only mission that works is one that the students have a hand in developing.

Armed with this mission, we began spreading awareness far and wide—"Did you know that The Leaning Eagle sources its milk locally? That it's better for you and the planet?" "Back by popular demand, The Leaning Eagle now rewards its customers with a loyalty program" (yes, that came back in an instant after our survey feedback. "Not all coffee is equal—is yours direct trade? Ours is." From Instagram posts to Twitter feeds to short chapel videos, we spread the word and, within a few weeks, were back to business as usual. All in all, the experience was insanely valuable for that group of students as an unplanned lesson in pivoting and rebranding. And it came together just in time for our CHCA Food Symposium.

After the success of the Food Symposium, things began moving at hyper-speed. First, I was invited to an event at the Stone Barns Center, home to Dan Barber's famous restaurant, Blue Hill at Stone Barns. The event brought educators from around the nation together to test out a food sustainability curriculum, so basically, I was in heaven. And as cool as the curriculum was, the *why* behind it was more impressive—changing the food system through a wide-scale educational initiative around equity and justice. As we were learning all about this curriculum, we were surrounded by rolling hills, pastured animals, and heirloom vegetables. Too good to be true—which could also be said about the meal I enjoyed at Blue Hill at Stone Barns on the last evening of the event.

During the final course (of more than I could count), I was served on the back patio near a blazing fire. The entire week had felt like something out of a fantasy designed specifically for my interests and in that moment, I knew that bringing this, in whatever possible form, to the students at CHCA would be essential. I wasn't sure if that meant tying it into English class, or working it into the entrepreneurship program, or creating an entirely new concept, but I knew that I had found my next mission. And on the plane ride back, as I was journaling the experience, I wrote two words that would go on to change the entire direction the entrepreneurship program as well as my role at the school: "teaching kitchen."

I spent the rest of the summer deep in research. What would it look like to develop a teaching kitchen on the school's campus? During the Food Symposium we had created a makeshift kitchen demonstration area in our commons space and it had been one of the highlights of the experience, so it seemed only natural to want to expand this into something much larger. A local farm in our area dedicated to organic growing methods and grass-raised livestock had just finished building a remarkable teaching kitchen and when I toured the facility, I learned that the build-out, which was housed out of an existing structure, cost north of $1 million. This, it seemed, would be my ask.

That August, during a well-intentioned but fundamentally flawed entire staff retreat, I found a few minutes alone with Dean to make my pitch. And I started guns blazing.

"Dean," I said, "I've got it. The next big idea."

"Oh?" he asked. "This will be good."

"Imagine this," I began. "The bell rings and you leave your geometry class to head to your next bell. Only instead of a traditional class, you head across the parking lot to a brand-new space where instead of textbooks and quizzes you have menus and cutting boards. Imagine creating a teaching kitchen right here on CHCA's campus."

"A teaching kitchen? I'm intrigued." Dean had always been a foodie and I knew this would speak directly to his own passions.

"It will be expensive," I said, "but I believe it will be worth every penny for the impact it will directly have on our students. All I need is $1 million."

He smiled.

"Seriously—this will be huge and it's the next step for the entrepreneurship program. I've already drawn up plans for what this could be and how it could function within the program."

"Speaking of entrepreneurship," he said, "I've been considering your role in the wake of the Food Symposium. The entrepreneurship program is certainly primed for growth. How would you feel about pursuing this full-time?"

"That was going to be my next question," I said. "I'm ready."

Dean and I began a series of meetings with the head of school, Randy Brunk, where we developed and outlined an entirely new role at the school. My pitch, which had developed over the last year through an awareness around sustainability, was to use this role change to rebrand the program as the Entrepreneurship and Sustainability Program. In my research regarding innovative programming at other schools, I found schools that had entrepreneurship programs and schools that had sustainability programs but none that had the two concepts brought together. And yet it seemed that the two concepts belonged together—if entrepreneurs are, in fact, problem solvers and if the problems our students would be facing in the next ten, twenty, and thirty years would be related to changing climate and limited natural resources, then it made sense that the two connect. Sustainability, however, was not connected solely to the environment—financial sustainability would be a key part of the program both in the way it would grow and in what it would teach. A final but immensely important aspect of sustainability involved health and wellness—the sustainability of the whole person. In a society that values hustle and nonstop activity, it would be important to help students live balanced lives.

I made my pitch to Randy and on the sustainability front, Dean jumped in to further the explanation: "I think we look at it from an inherently Christ-centered perspective," he said. "We are called to be stewards of the earth, which is the essence of sustainability. We just had Joel Salatin, a Christian farmer, on campus talking about Christians needing to step up and demand change—well here's our chance. We can embrace sustainability as a school."

Randy enthusiastically nodded his agreement. I was given a three-year pilot program and told that if the program took off and was successful, I'd be off to the races, and if it crashed and burned, I'd still be able to move back into full-time classroom teaching. Three years to prove the concept—three years to build something amazing.

And just like that, the Entrepreneurship and Sustainability Program was born.

CHAPTER SIX

"The entrepreneurship program at CHCA demonstrated the qualities required of a leader. I was able to take what I was learning in the classroom and practically apply it at the coffee bar every day. The program allowed for a future where I could become an entrepreneur myself."

— Kennedy, '21

"Dean," I began, several months into my new position, "what kind of money do you still have in your budget for professional development?"

Despite the rush of events that was the growth of the entrepreneurship program, I was still fixated on the idea of a kitchen space where students could learn culinary arts, food sustainability, and even start businesses. It seemed a perfect fit for entrepreneurship, but I had to figure out where to start. Of course, the concept of home economics had been around for ages, but this was something new—this was more about where the food came from, its nutritional components, and its connection to wellness.

All of this had led me to an intriguing annual convention called "Healthy Kitchens, Healthy Lives." Jointly put on by Harvard University's T. H. Chan School of Public Health and the Culinary Institute of America, this event drew in wellness operators, hospital administrators, university professors, and medical practitioners. Over the course of three days at the campus of the Culinary Institute of America (CIA), this event promised to dive into the *why* behind teaching kitchens and their influence on nutrition. Plus, it was in Napa. I made a fervent case for attending and set off in early February 2020 to discover the path ahead.

I arrived in Napa the evening before the start of the convention and checked into my Airbnb, which was a tiny home nestled in a quiet cul-de-sac just outside of the downtown area. To counter any potential jet lag, I rose early in the morning and went for a run along the riverfront area. As I was rounding the corner of a circuitous running path, I reentered the main street just as the sun was rising. Ahead of me was the famous Oxbow Market and the early morning vendors bustled in and out of the building as I ran by. Just past the market is Copia—the former American Center for Wine, Food & the Arts, now the Culinary Institute of America. I stood in the courtyard and surveyed the building that would consume my waking hours for the next few days.

It was vastly unlike the traditional convention center with its myriad entrances and exits and airport-like feel of sterile uniformity. The courtyard was lined with avocado and fig trees while raised-bed gardens dotted the scenery. A nearby bridge arched over the Napa River and the early morning chill in the air added to the intoxicating feel. It wasn't just the California scenery or the proximity to world-renowned vineyards that added to the feeling of anticipation—it was the sense that I belonged. Here was a place where food was sacred, and locally grown wasn't just a branding campaign. Here existed a utopia of sustainability and flavor and wholeness. And here I was, drinking it all in.

If I had any lingering suspicion that the next three days would not deliver on the now incredibly high expectations from the event, they were quickly dissipated within the opening session. Dr. David Eisenberg took the stage, which was placed just in front of a demonstration kitchen. His opening welcome promised insightful research, delicious food, and inspiring speakers. He discussed the hands-on experiences to be had in the kitchen labs and the networking events around wine tastings. He highlighted the impressive caliber of the speakers addressing a range of nutritional research and how their presentations would be supplemented with chefs demonstrating key recipes and techniques that would then be featured in the expansive breakfast and lunch offerings. And the event was nothing short of spectacular. From session to session, I went from inspired to overwhelmed to encouraged to challenged. I tasted food that blew my mind and learned more about nutrition than I ever deemed possible. But most of all, I saw, firsthand, the impact a teaching kitchen could have.

I was hooked. But I was also out of place.

As far as I could tell, I was officially the only person present at the event not affiliated with a major university or hospital. My name tag, which clearly read "Cincinnati Hills Christian Academy" initiated many questions about what sort of institution I was with and when I explained I was representing a K–12 school, I was met with questioning glances and confused looks. One speaker, who I had tracked down to pepper with questions following his talk on the current research on red meat, asked me what university I was with.

"I'm with a K–12 school in Cincinnati, Ohio," I said.

"K–12? Like elementary and high school?"

I nodded.

"Well, what are *you* doing *here*?" he asked in surprise.

The three days passed in a happy stupor of information overload and although I didn't know where to start, I knew I was sufficiently moved to take the teaching kitchen world by storm. I was ready to return to Cincinnati and beg for the money to start a kitchen. I was willing to build a kitchen with my own two hands—though, for those familiar with my handiwork, this would have been a lose-lose for everyone involved.

I was on fire—and mostly because of the Teaching Kitchen Collaborative (TKC). The TKC had been formed by Dr. David Eisenberg in 2016 to connect the network of organizations around the world that were using teaching kitchens to teach concepts of health and wellness across all settings (universities, wellness centers, hospitals, etc.). And the TKC was leading the charge of wellness education built around nutrition principles that was taking the world by storm. Joined by organizations like Stanford University, Google, and Compass Group, this collaborative had an impressive list of members and was striving for systematic change on multiple levels. As the conference began to wind to a close, a vision began to materialize in my mind— Cincinnati Hills Christian Academy would build a teaching kitchen as part of the entrepreneurship and sustainability program, and we would join the TKC as their first K–12 school. We would work to build nutritional awareness and holistic wellness into our programming and show that a key aspect of the entrepreneurial mindset is related to wellness.

Everything began to make sense—the carbon footprint awareness at the coffee bar, the Food Symposium event, the excitement around innovative learning. Everything was moving toward our next key step: creating a teaching kitchen.

My brain was in a state of excitement and clarity when Dr. David Eisenberg took the stage for the closing statements of the three-day event. I was furiously scribbling notes, diagramming the blueprint of our future kitchen space and dreaming of the new build-out and how it would be accomplished, when Dr. Eisenberg directly addressed the crowd.

"Friends," he said, "it is my custom at the end of this precious annual event to allow time for those among you who wish to say something. Perhaps you wish to share a dream or a desire or something that you learned and want to take back. I invite you to come to the front where you can speak into the microphone. Now is the time."

Perhaps it was my own fundamentalist upbringing with a deeply ingrained culture of altar calls that grabbed me in that moment, but in a seemingly possessed state, I found myself moving quickly toward the front of the room. As I neared the microphone, the world seemed to slow down, and I became filled with a passion to share the dream.

"I just want to say," I said, leaning down into the microphone and scanning the room, "thank you. First, for letting me spend the last three days in your company—as a high school educator, I am thoroughly out of my depth in a crowd such as this. I do not teach at a university or run a hospital or facilitate a wellness center.

I am not a chef or a registered dietician. And yet you've let me sit among you and learn. Which is the second thing I'm thankful for—inspiration.

"I came here to learn the ins and outs of what it would look like to have a dedicated kitchen space in our school but what I learned instead was far more important. I learned *why* we need a dedicated kitchen space, *why* the concept of the teaching kitchen is so powerful, and *why* every school across the nation needs to have one. In short, I have become inspired. And that is *why*," I said, pausing to take a breath, "that is *why* I am returning to Cincinnati, Ohio, where we *will* build a teaching kitchen and we *will* educate our students on the concepts of nutrition and wellness, and we *will* return here and join the Teaching Kitchen Collaborative. Thank you."

I moved to return to my seat, feeling the dual emotions that often accompany an impromptu outburst of speech—pride at having seized the opportunity and regret at what I may have said in my state of excitement. The time for these emotions was short-lived, however, as my way became blocked by Dr. David Eisenberg himself. As he moved toward me, I immediately assumed the worst—I had been found out as an imposter and he was going to kick me out of the assembly and ensure we would never be able to return.

Instead, he reached out his arms and enveloped me in a hug. Yes, a literal hug. The man responsible for the entire convention, for working to build momentum toward a national movement of change was standing in front of the auditorium hugging me. So, I hugged him back.

Dr. Eisenberg then moved to the microphone and, with tears forming in his eyes, addressed the crowd.

"Many of you may not know this," he began, "but from the beginning, from the very start of this movement, it was my goal to get Teaching Kitchens into schools. Into education. And not just any education, but elementary and high school education. If we are going to spark change in the way we treat nutrition and wellness, it must start as early as possible," he said, pausing to look around the room. "And my new friend here"—he turned to look at my name tag—"Stephen Carter, is going to do just that. Stephen, thank *you*."

Applause thundered through the room as Dr. Eisenberg stepped down and put his hand on my shoulder.

"Stephen," he said, away from the microphone and looking directly at me, "it usually takes about three years to complete the process of kitchen and program build-out. Let me know when you are ready, and I would be overjoyed to welcome you into the Teaching Kitchen Collaborative."

Out of the corner of my eye, I could see Caerus gearing up to run by, his long lock of hair flowing as he swayed from side to side. This was opportunity, as pure as ever. Opportunity to engage students in the learning experience on an even larger level. Chasing opportunity is not for the light of heart or for those who dream small. Chasing opportunity is about seizing it in the here and now and committing to the ride.

For these reasons, I looked straight back at Dr. Eisenberg and said, "Sir, that may be the case, but you'll be hearing from me in half that time."

He smiled his warm, generous smile and said, "Stephen, I knew I liked you."

On my way back to my Airbnb, I was walking higher than the clouds. The dream had been realized not just by me, but by Dr. Eisenberg himself. We were on a path toward something much larger than any of us had realized when we first rolled that coffee cart down the hallway to sell a student-made latte. Yes, we had a tremendous amount of work ahead of us and yes, we now had a rather intensive goal of doing so in a year and a half, but the excitement was electrifying.

And it was in this state that I answered a phone call from my wife.

"Hey, babe," she said, the slightest twinge of concern notable in her voice, "what time does your flight leave?"

"Later tonight—it's a redeye. Why?"

"You might want to consider wearing a mask in the airport," she said.

"No, I don't think so," I said, preparing myself for one of her usual lectures on whatever fear-mongering news story she had recently read. "This is about the whole coronavirus thing? You're worried for no reason."

"It's getting to be a bigger issue," she said, "and I simply think if you're flying out of San Francisco, you should wear a mask. That's all."

"Fine," I said, a little too sharply. "Fine. I'll see you tomorrow morning. And I have *a lot* to tell you about."

"I look forward to it," she said, a smile now detectable in her tone. "See you tomorrow."

Within two months, the world shut down.

CHAPTER SEVEN

> *"The entrepreneurship program provided a hands-on learning experience that fostered confidence to take on new challenges, critical thinking skills, and effective communication. Mastering these skills in high school prepared me for a successful college and post-grad experience."*
>
> — Candace, '18

It's hard to imagine a larger catalyst for change than the global pandemic. The world became dominated overnight with the mentality of fear, loss, and survival. And the weight of the unknown was itself, at times, unbearable. Will this ever end? Will my loved ones survive? Will the world return to normal? These were the questions that now dominated our lives. And these sorts of questions can irrevocably change a person's outlook. Businesses saw this firsthand—workers were laid off, operations shut down, and revenues diminished. The entire system we had collectively relied on and taken for granted for decades had been turned upside down.

The effect on education is still being researched and documented. From the pivots teachers made to offer online learning to the facilitation of classroom atmospheres on Zoom, education was rocked to its core. And in many ways, the entire educational system became a microcosm of the world. Despite the hardship and horrible conditions of COVID, it did bring to the surface several key issues that had been buried for some time. It brought us face-to-face with the changing shape of education today—we had to account for teaching practices from ages past designed to train students for industries no longer in existence. We had to reconcile our outdated practices with a society that allowed only for the absolutely necessary in information transfer. We had to think outside the box, to look for hidden opportunities, to willingly retrain ourselves to retrain our students. We had to try and fail and try again and do this over and over with no promising end in sight. We had, in other words, to think and act like entrepreneurs.

COVID exposed an educational system in disarray and, like a scab torn the skin, forced us to heal and regrow. And perhaps the greatest (possibly only) gift from the pandemic was time—we were given an abundance of time. Work was remote, in-person connections and networking ceased to exist, and our office hours shifted astronomically. Suddenly, we were faced with an excess of a finite resource we had previously written off as never having again. We became bored, we took up inane hobbies, we read books, we tried writing books, we cooked, we started playing musical instruments, and scoured the Internet for useless information. We watched entire seasons of shows in a single sitting, and we found the time to connect with relatives (virtually) more than ever before. It was as if a reset button had been pressed and we were now able to choose, for better or worse, how to spend the minutes of our lives.

It would be deeply offensive to ever suggest that COVID was a blessing, but it is undeniable that it presented us with a rich bed of newfound opportunity through the gift of time. And this gift of time provided the spark that would end up fast-tracking the growth of the entrepreneurship program in an exponential manner. And this growth must be attributed to embracing a "learner" mindset over a "learned" mindset. I discovered, quite by accident, that I had been operating day to day with a learned mindset. I felt qualified to oversee the coffee bar because I knew and understood the programming. I felt qualified to run a food symposium because I was "learned" in those processes. What I ended up discovering was what John Maxwell refers to as the Law of the Lid—I had inadvertently capped the potential growth of the program through my own limitations as a leader.

All my learning, up to this point, had been related to English. The success of the coffee bar and the beginning phases of the entrepreneurship program had been directly tied to my own passions and I had worked to pull students into those areas. But I was learned, not a learner. This was a difficult realization because I had always considered myself to be a person with a growth mindset, but my growth had become stagnant. Prolific author and philosopher Eric Hoffer explained the difference between the learner and the learned this way: "In a world of change, the learners shall inherit the earth, while the learned shall find themselves perfectly suited for a world that no longer exists." This statement rings truer today than when Hoffer first uttered it. COVID pushed us into a new world where those of us who were "learned" were no longer suited. Only those who were willing to become active "learners" would thrive, and we had every tool at our disposal to do so. Best of all, we now had the time.

I took advantage of this immediately. Multiple times over the past years I had been given opportunities to take part in small group business coaching, but I had never had the time (or so I said as an excuse). Now I had the time—and I dove in. I discovered that I was, in fact, hungry to learn. A business coach in our school community invited me to join his virtual class for an eight-week program designed to fast-track entrepreneurial success. Over the course of the Zoom sessions, reading materials, and personalized coaching, I received a life lesson that put both me and the entire entrepreneurship program on a fast track for growth: *It's acceptable to need a coach.* This was a groundbreaking realization. Coaching had, for me, been relegated to the arena of high school sports and club athletics and for anyone in my position to need a coach was to admit to being smaller than desired. The realization, for me, was that I could become larger through admitting I was smaller.

A giddiness for learning began to permeate my every day. For the first time since I had been in graduate classes, I fell in love with being a student and with the pure, unadulterated pursuit of knowledge. A newfound passion for reading nonfiction began to develop. The bulk of my reading over the last fifteen years had been fiction literature and I had largely scoffed at "success literature." Now I began devouring it. First was Simon Sinek's *Start with Why*, which I finished and then promptly read again. This led to *The E-Myth Revisited*; *Atomic Habits*; *The New One Minute Manager*; *Developing the Leaders Around You*; *Change Your Questions, Change Your Life*; *The Goal*; *Good to Great*; *How to Win*

Friends and Influence People; The Vision Driven Leader; The Infinite Game; Building a Story Brand; Blue Ocean Strategy; The Five Dysfunctions of a Team; The Ideal Team Player; Think and Grow Rich; and *The Magic of Thinking Big*. I was feasting on some of the greatest concepts developed by some of the greatest thinkers and I was thrust headfirst into the world of personal growth.

From as early as I can remember, I've been a goal-oriented person. When I was entering fifth grade, I took my entire savings of $300 and spent it on a used Honda lawnmower. I pushed this up and down my street and built a business that I operated until college. The hustle and the grind are second nature to my character—it's hard to remember a time when I wasn't working toward some financial or intellectual or vocational goal. My journey of goal setting and habit formation became firmly solidified in my life and I would spend the next seventeen years developing these skills. But they would, for the most part, remain dormant. This dormancy, however, ended abruptly in the spring of 2020.

As I continued with my voracious reading, I came across what would become the most influential book of my life: Stephen Covey's famous work, *The Seven Habits of Highly Effective People*. I had a colorful history with this book having first purchased it during a stint working at a bookstore at age twenty-two. I started reading it, gave up, put it on the shelf, returned to it a few years later, started reading it, gave up again. This time I started reading it with a different mindset—one forged out of a desire to learn and soak up every possible teaching I could on living the effective life. And Covey delivered. I finished the book and immediately purchased the audiobook (which Covey himself reads) so I could experience it once again. There are few books that I take the time to reread, but there and then I made the commitment to reread *The Seven Habits* every year and I have found each time that it opens new concepts and sharpens my growth—it actively keeps me as a "learner" and not a "learned."

Covey's principles are timeless and his strategies to fulfill the principles work. The takeaway that has been most valuable for the entrepreneurship program is his emphasis on the Eisenhower Matrix. For those unfamiliar with the workings of this matrix, the concept is as follows: Your time is made of hours in a day and days in a week and weeks in a month. These months make up your years, which in turn make up your life. In life, we often have big, overarching goals and large projects we want to tackle and while we mean well, often the day-to-day craziness eats at our time until none is left. If too many days are caught up in the whirlwind (the concept coined by Chris McChesney, Jim Huling, and Sean Covey in *The 4 Disciplines of Execution*), which refers to the controlled (or uncontrolled) chaos of the everyday that hits us through email, meetings, and inane activities, then our weeks begin to fill, which then fill our months and then fill our years. Before too long, we are looking back at a life of unfulfilled potential and wondering where all the time went to accomplish the goals and dreams we set out to conquer.

Enter the Eisenhower Matrix. The matrix is divided into four quadrants and each quadrant has a clearly defined label. In the top left corner is our "urgent and important" quadrant. These items include turning in those expense reports and grading semester exams. These are the items that have to be done and need to be bumped up on the priority list. When we get an email with the "high urgency" alert, this is the quadrant being referenced. The quadrant directly below it is the "urgent and not important" quadrant. These are the items that often masquerade as important but in fact, are not. These are the items that, if left untended, will resolve themselves. These are the emails asking for additional information and the requests to meet for issues outside your circle of urgency. These are activities that may seem important at the time but are designed solely to pull you away from meeting your goals. Thus enters the top right quadrant—this is the quadrant that, according to Covey, we should strive to live in. This quadrant is aptly named "not urgent and important" and this is where we put our dreams and our goals and our ambitions. This is where we list the books we want to write and the lessons we want to plan and the vacations we want to go on. This is where we mention starting a podcast and building a website. These are the things that, looking back, add the most value and meaning to our lives but are not, in the moment, urgent. As a result, roughly 90 percent of the population never even enters this quadrant because of the tractor-beam-like pull of the two urgent quadrants.

It is not possible to live a life where we completely ignore the first quadrant, urgent and important. Or at least not a life where you maintain a steady job and paycheck. But there is a life, and a rich one indeed, where we ignore the second quadrant, "urgent and not important," as well as the fourth quadrant, "not urgent and not important." These are the areas that suck our time and leave us with nothing to pursue that which is truly important. In the last category, you find things like "spend thirty minutes scrolling through TikTok" or "updating my Facebook friends on my weekend's activities" or "reading all the comments from my last social media post." These are things that are neither urgent nor important but exist solely to distract you from your dreams. The epiphany from Covey comes when we realize that everything we want in life is possible and entirely within the realm of realism if we learn to manage our time according to prioritization.

In his work, this principle is referred to as "put first things first" and it is truly central to the effective life, which means understanding the roots of prioritization so that you focus on the wildly important. His son, Sean Covey, would go on to expound upon this with McChesney and Huling in clearly defining the Wildly Important Goal (WIG). These Wildly Important Goals are only accomplishable when we create a daily and therefore weekly schedule that gives us enough time in the second quadrant. Where the genius of the Eisenhower Matrix comes into play is in the planning of our week. We can sit down at the start of each seven days and literally plan out when we will work on the high-level, quadrant three activities. This works directly in tandem with the famous Pareto principle. The Pareto principle, popularly known as the 80/20 rule, suggests that 80 percent of results come from 20 percent of activities. In other words, 80 percent of your sales, in a business, come from 20 percent of your customers. Eighty percent of your satisfaction in life comes from the way in which you use 20 percent of our time. The principle suggests that if we examine our lives by the 80/20 rule, we can exponentially maximize effectiveness by increasing our attention on the 20 percent. If 80 percent of your sales are coming from 20 percent of your customers, double down on those customers (and create a customer avatar to find more of them) to increase your overall sales.

The principle is true in our lives. The third quadrant, "not urgent but important" is our 20 percent (or our 25%, since it is a quadrant). This is the quadrant of our time where we get the most out of our time. Time spent working on these big goals is time that will be maximized through our own satisfaction as well as our overall accomplishment in life. It means we have to spend less time in the other quadrants (fewer inane meetings? sign me up!) but sacrifice is always necessary to achieve greatness. And this plays directly into the entrepreneurial mindset. If we are to set our minds to seek opportunities, redefine failure, and try to carve out a meaningful existence using our finite time, we cannot say yes to everything. Knowing when and in what circumstances to say no is central to our productivity and therefore to our sense of satisfaction in life. For these reasons and more, Covey's work completely transformed my thinking over a few short months as I was working toward a total and complete renaissance in my thinking and time management.

This renaissance was directly connected to the explosive growth the entrepreneurship program experienced starting in the spring of 2020. As the world settled into a new normal, the program began to pick up momentum through a number of exciting developments. Perhaps the best way to explain this development is through the metaphor of the flywheel. Used by Jim Collins in *Good to Great*, the flywheel is the perfect representation of the start-up, entrepreneurship model. The flywheel is a massive wheel on an axle that requires an extreme amount of force to begin moving. That extreme force is applied in a constant stream until, finally, the wheel begins to turn. As the wheel turns, it picks up momentum and then it slowly begins to require less force to continue to turn. More and more revolutions of the wheel take place and the wheel moves faster each time, picking up speed and picking up power. After a while, the flywheel rolls along nicely requiring just a small dose of force to continue its movement.

It is often at this point that an onlooker will appear, observe the wheel, and ask how the wheel is spinning so quickly with so little force. The onlooker will conclude that you must "have the magic touch" or that the wheel "is not as hard to turn as it appears." This is because there is an innate desire for all of us to not recognize the amount of work required to start a movement. Sam Walton, in his famous autobiography *Made in America*, explains this phenomenon in a tongue-in-cheek manner: "And like most other overnight successes, it was about twenty years in the making." Those who look at the success of the entrepreneurship program at Cincinnati Hills Christian Academy often fall into this trap—seeing the elective courses and the numerous businesses and the beautiful spaces and the student engagement and thinking, "Wow, how lucky are they that they had all of this overnight success." In fact, it was the continued force, applied slowly and over time through dedication and persistence, through a concerted focus on living in the third quadrant, putting first things first, and understanding the necessity of prioritizing. The flywheel had been established when the coffee bar came into existence, but it was the rebirth of learning during COVID that applied the necessary force to start the wheel turning. Once it was turning, it was time to hang on for the ride of our lives.

CHAPTER EIGHT

"This entrepreneurship program taught me crucial collaborative and organizational skills that I still use today. It also brought together a wide group of people who formed friendships that continue to this day."

— Connor, '16

Wild rides, it turns out, are often made possible through wild goals. Those wild goals are only attainable with wild systems that are carried out with wild dedication. Much of the success of the entrepreneurship and sustainability program is due to an unrelenting intentionality toward the goal-setting process. And the overarching lesson of the entire goal-setting process, learned the hard but necessary way, is that the goal always needs to be larger. As I write these words, I'm reflecting back on the original goal sheet I worked up in the spring of 2020 as I considered the future of the program. Included in that list of "dream big goals" was hire someone to help grow the program, build a fully commercial teaching kitchen, start a podcast, and raise $100,000 for program growth. These were goals that, at the moment, seemed far off and elusive but big enough to cause daily motivation. And it's true, they caused daily motivation. But every single one of them (and many more) would be accomplished within fifteen months. These days, when I'm asked what it is that I do, I share the mission that defines my *why*: I am laboring to develop the entrepreneurial mindset in all learners, so they are radically transformed to impact their lives.

It was through the goal-setting process (and breaking these goals into yearlong, ninety-day, sixty-day, and thirty-day segments) that I came to understand the necessity of connecting goals to core values. It was one thing to say, "I want to read fifty-two books a year" as a goal but if that goal was not inherently tied to something intrinsically of worth to the goal-setter, its accomplishment would mean nothing in the end. Core values define us and they are a clear reflection of our *why*. Understanding our *why* is the process of defining our personal mission statement—a worthy activity everyone should undertake. Just as a business wants to have a clearly defined *why* and mission statement, so too should the individual. Sinek's *Start with Why* can be just as easily applied to our own lives. When people look at us or meet us or engage us in conversation, what do they take away? What sort of person do we project onto the world? Taking the time to clearly analyze this is essential to building a healthy goal-setting process.

This is also how we move from a "job" or "the work I do" into the realm of "calling" and "purpose." Connecting our inherent *why* to the work of our lives is the key to finding purpose and fulfillment. The salesperson associated with Sweetwater (a company specializing in musical instruments, pro audio, and accessories) is directly associated with selling microphones and audio equipment. But if we dig into the *why* behind this, we discover that this individual is actually in the business of giving people a voice. It just so happens that he also sells microphones. There is great power in this type of thinking and most importantly, it empowers those who may currently find little to no sense of purpose in their work. It also leads to clarity in the ways in which our work reflects our personal values.

This deep dive into core values became the driving force to both understand and then articulate the core values not just of myself but of the burgeoning entrepreneurship and sustainability program at CHCA. And more specifically, the core values that made up the entrepreneurial mindset. In this journey to uncover what is really meant by the entrepreneurial mindset, I discovered that I was seeking not values but attributes. The distinction is often hazy, but clarity was provided in the following—values guide our goals and direction while attributes are the operational mechanisms we use to meet those goals. Simple Google searches turned up more than fifty primary attributes included in the entrepreneurial mindset. I imagined standing in front of parents and students while listing these fifty attributes and explaining how they were all essential to the entrepreneurial mindset. The truth is, fifty attributes is about forty-five too many.

Thus began a journey to truly understand what was required to think like an entrepreneur. And this journey led to insight around not what we wanted to instill but what was already being instilled. In other words, it merely gave us language to explain the learning that was already happening. And it all started with growth mindset. Growth mindset, or the belief that our abilities can be improved through focus and effort, is truly foundational to the entire concept of thinking like an entrepreneur. The alternative is a fixed mindset, and we all know where that leads.

Once growth mindset is in place, it leads to the development of grit, the ability to redefine failure, and the intrinsic ability to seek opportunities. These four attributes, growth mindset, grit, redefining failure, and opportunity seeking, became the driving focus of our attention—the metric by which we measured our success.

While the second part of this book will dive deeply into each of these attributes, it is worth noting that the entire story of the program's creation reflects an intertwined weaving of these values throughout since its inception. Once these were clearly defined on paper, however, the growth of the program took on an intensity and focus that previously did not exist. The irony was that in simplifying, limiting, and clarifying our approach, our growth became magnified. Such is the case in life—when we become intentionally intentional by narrowing our focus, our results yield exponential returns. The question I get most often from schools is, "How do I find the right person to lead this kind of programming?" There are many answers to this, but at the core, the right person is the person whose personal values and driving sense of purpose are in complete alignment with the intended direction of the program. This allows for a beautiful interweaving of purpose, calling, and fulfillment, the fruit of which will be extraordinary student engagement and incredible program growth.

And growth begets growth. As soon as I clearly defined my *why*, my mission statement, and my core values, I continued my journey as learner and discovered a need to seek out mentors. Part of this realization came from my foray into "automobile university"—a term coined by motivational Zig Ziglar. We all have the opportunity to attend automobile university simply by choosing what we listen to when in the car. The average American spends one hour a day in the car which, over the course of a month, is enough time to listen to about three entire audiobooks. Over the course of a year, that's about thirty-six books. Over a lifetime, that's a whole library. I had long been an advocate of audiobooks and lectures and event podcasts while driving, but it was around this time that my automobile university turned to famous business guru of times past, Jim Rohn. Jim has countless hours of incredible audio content and one of the echoing precepts he clearly articulates is the need for mentorship. This notion is a topic expressed with equal passion by leadership expert John Maxwell. In his *15 Invaluable Laws of Personal Growth*, Maxwell lays out a clear and effective plan for mentorship: Make a list of the people you want to learn from, then ask them out to dinner (and be sure to pay for their meal) and while you are eating, pepper them with questions on everything you want to know. Take solid notes and transfer these notes to your permanent journal after the fact. In doing this, you affirm the mentor and his/her gift of time, and you also solidify the learnings.

I wasted no time in procuring a long list of mentors and, mostly through Zoom as we were still in the midst of COVID, I worked through a plan to learn as much as possible from those whose experience spoke loudly and clearly. Soon it was a full-time business of taking and transcribing notes from these calls so that the material could be assimilated and then distilled to the students in the program. The current problem, of course, was that there were no students meeting in person. In fact, one could have argued, there was no entrepreneurship program currently. Unlike traditional classes, like English or social studies, the entrepreneurship program did not have a clear-cut method to move into the virtual world. The twenty-four coffee bar managers all had different bells of the day assigned to their entrepreneurship internship, so corralling them all for synchronous learning was difficult.

Like all problems, though, this was really an opportunity in disguise. If I was connecting with mentors on Zoom and by phone and then taking that information and using it to develop curriculum for entrepreneurship, then why not skip a few steps and record these sessions? If recording these sessions, then why not make them widely available to the students? If making these widely available to the students, then why not start a podcast? Within two weeks, the CHCA Entrepreneurial Podcast was born.

Throughout the first semester of 2020, as the world was pivoting and certain industries were collapsing, students in CHCA's entrepreneurship program held class in a most nontraditional manner. Each week, they were tasked with listening to the latest podcast and then engaging in an ongoing online discussion forum where they applied the topics from the podcast to The Leaning Eagle Coffee Bar. They worked on their own time and came up with a wealth of ideas and plans to put into place once the business could reopen. One of the ideas that came up in the online discussion forum was a direct-to-home coffee bean mailing service to "keep customers happy during the shutdown." Although the plan was not a huge success, their quick implantation of it represented the sort of prototyping and market testing mentality that would lead to the program's ongoing growth. And it kept us all connected despite the uncertainty.

Meanwhile, I plugged away at developing large goals for where the program would go. The biggest of these, of course, was the teaching kitchen. Although a little traction had been developed right after the Healthy Kitchens, Healthy Lives conference, the current state of things made any movement toward building a physical kitchen problematic. Once again, however, the problem was an opportunity in disguise. Fresh off the success of the launch of the podcast, it made sense to begin rallying community support around the idea of a culinary aspect to entrepreneurship. While I had shared the idea of the teaching kitchen with a few people at the school, I had yet to spread the news widely to our entire school population. And what better way to rally support than to get people excited about cooking.

COVID was a boon to the at-home culinary world—people with no previous experience in the kitchen were sampling recipes and learning how to bake, braise, roast, and sauté. Interest in baking was through the roof and access to flour, yeast, rice, and other fundamentals was limited. As the world shut down, the ovens turned on. To capitalize on this excitement and begin paving the way for an eventual teaching kitchen (in other words, to begin raising funding), a YouTube channel was launched. Now, before you begin conjuring notions of a grand, wide-scale launch that drew national attention (remember John Krasinski's *Some Good News?*), the CHCA Teaching Kitchen YouTube channel maxed out at one hundred subscribers. Still, however, it was the perfect way to get people excited about what was to come.

The channel started with a variety of short videos featuring a range of techniques (chopping garlic, making smoothies, baking bread) and lectures (why local food, getting started in the kitchen, etc.) To generate even more excitement, I pivoted to live videos hosted weekly where anyone in the community could join in and cook alongside the featured chef. This garnered even more excitement when guest alumni began to teach culinary skills including perfectly created chocolate chip cookies and New York-style bagels. With each episode, it felt as if we were getting closer and closer to making the dream a reality.

CHAPTER NINE

"The entrepreneurship program at CHCA was the highlight of my high school career. Mr. Carter's program offered experimental learning that not only instilled within me the understanding of how to successfully operate a business on a large and day-to-day scale, but it also allowed me to meet some of the most influential people in my life."

— Megan, '19

If Caerus had consistently been running past since the start of the entrepreneurship program, he chose the time period of COVID to do daily wind sprints. Every problem that surfaced brought opportunities galore and the difficulty became not the lack of options but rather which ones were worth exploring. As we neared the end of the school year and began making plans both for remote and in-person learning, not knowing which would be our reality in the fall, teachers began making decisions about whether or not to continue at the school. It was during this period of uncertainty that I learned about a shift in our environmental sciences programming.

The environmental sciences program was housed in our beautiful four-thousand-square-foot greenhouse that had been built as a result of the school's Light the Way campaign in 2018.

The greenhouse boasted fully automated systems with a cooling wall, gas heaters, and circulation fans. Built onto the back of the greenhouse was a two-thousand-square-foot, unfinished space that was currently being used as a makeshift classroom. The teacher who had been instrumental in building the program and the space was leaving to take a job in a different industry, which left the school with a remarkable greenhouse and no greenhouse instructor.

"Dean," I said, over a Zoom call (which by May had become second nature), "I have an idea."

By this point in the journey, Dean was prepared for any number of things when I started with "I have an idea." And most telling of all, he was prepared to tell me that I wouldn't be able to get the money I was asking for.

"And," I continued, sensing the hesitation, "it doesn't cost the school anything."

I proceeded to lay out a plan. In a moment of inspiration, the entire future of the program had become clear during a routine walk around the neighborhood. This entire time I had been waiting for a large financial gift that would enable us to build a stand-alone teaching kitchen, but all along, the space for the kitchen had already been built—and it was built on the back of the school's greenhouse. The existing unfinished space would be perfect for the formal build-out of a commercial kitchen and having it attached to such a gorgeous growing space further fueled my excitement. And driving all of this excitement was the knowledge that if student engagement was a primary driver of success, then this was the path to get there.

Going back to the Food Symposium, this passion around locally sourced food and understanding where one's food came from had taken me on a journey toward "Farm to School Programming." However, Farm to School programming, while terrific, rarely involved the actual cooking of the food once it was grown. Imagine a program that was both farm-to-school and school-to-plate—a complete circle of nutrition and wellness. And the entire nexus was already built and recently vacated.

I shared the vision with Dean—the space would be transformed into a showcase of educational programming around horticulture. Tomatoes would be trellised from the floor to the ceiling, a lettuce pond would produce extraordinary amounts of bibb and romaine varieties, and an entire series of tower gardens would turn over vast amounts of produce monthly. Elementary classes would come through the space to learn about food and gardening and harvesting. They would leave excited about food and starting seeds and this excitement would carry over into all parts of their education.

It helped my case that for the last several months, my family and I had taken over care of the school's raised-bed garden. The garden, built by a graduating senior, had flourished for several years before falling into disrepair. In seeking a family-friendly, outdoor activity during COVID, my wife and kids and I had started tending to the garden. We spent hours each week carefully weeding and tending to the seedlings until the space resembled its glory days of the past. I had already been planning on weaving academic programming into this raised-bed garden space once school returned to in-person, so upon hearing about the opening in the greenhouse, the larger move just made sense.

Dean was on board and gave me the full go-ahead and within two weeks, the entrepreneurship program headquarters (consisting of myself and a few stacks of books) moved into the unfinished space on the back of the greenhouse. The space was cluttered with tables, chairs, shelving, and plant supplies—it was a work in progress, and a massive undertaking for only the craziest of individuals. It just so happened, however, that the craziest of individuals was now looking around and seeing not a mess nor a disaster but instead the future home of the official CHCA Teaching Kitchen. And it was beautiful indeed.

Not to mention a massive undertaking. Now that we were fully immersed in the greenhouse and now that there were plans to build a teaching kitchen in the unfinished space, it was time to pull in student interest. Although there was still a great deal of uncertainty about in-person classes in the fall of 2020, we were making plans regardless. I started with the horticulture and agriculture programming. The space was already there—the raised-bed garden was flourishing and the greenhouse was ready to go. It was tangible—students could see where they would be working and they could easily picture the type of work. For this reason, getting twelve students to agree to the project was not difficult. I structured a class designed like the coffee bar where students would participate in a yearlong internship. Unlike the coffee bar, however, I made this class meet during one specific bell of the day. This way, those students could work directly with me as we developed a horticulture program.

I am not a believer in coincidence—I believe in things happening because they were meant to happen. This is why, when the upper school's leadership team chose to divert our regular eight bell schedule into a permanent block schedule (four bells per day), I chose to rejoice. This meant I would have a full eighty minutes with my students in the greenhouse and it would give us considerably more time to dive into projects. The plan was rolled out as a pilot for the 2020–2021 school year and included opportunities for late arrival and early dismissal in order to limit the number of students in the building at any one time. It would be reevaluated at the end of the year, but for now, we would have longer bells and more time to work.

And work we did. These students dove in with gusto and tackled projects far beyond the scope of a high school class. We were given funding from our auxiliary account to purchase supplies for the greenhouse space, and our first purchase was a block of ten vertical tower gardens. These tower gardens, first introduced to me through an engaging and helpful participant in the Food Symposium, were perfect for our greenhouse. Each one held room for forty-four total plants and yet the footprint of the entire tower was the space where traditionally one could only grow about eight plants. In other words, the towers enabled us to maximize and exponentially increase what we would be able to produce in the same space. It also automated the process as the towers are each connected to one main irrigation line that feeds in the proper nutrient blend.

The day these towers arrived, which was in mid-July 2020, I assembled the students and, working outside in a socially distanced manner, we encountered a crash course in assembling aeroponic units. And the finished result (with the exception of one or two leaning towers) was impressive. It also made for a great Facebook post. It's worth noting that a good deal of the successful advertisement of the entrepreneurship and sustainability program comes from social media. At CHCA, as with many schools, parents are inundated with information from weekly newsletters to text alerts to email bombardment. As a result, most parents tune out information from the school, making communication around new projects intensely difficult.

Social media posts, however, featuring pictures of students engaged, smiling, and using their hands never fails to arouse parental enthusiasm. It is also how we keep the community in the know regarding our ever-expanding program and the ways in which their children can get involved. And when it comes to ever-expanding, the fall of 2020 was truly the semester when the floodgates of progress opened for entrepreneurship programming. And they opened with such force that we were almost drowned. At the same time, I was launching the horticulture program within entrepreneurship, I began soliciting a group of students to help launch the culinary program by helping to build the elusive teaching kitchen. While staffing the horticulture group was not difficult, it was considerably harder to convince a group of high schoolers to give up on one of their bells for a project they could neither see nor fully understand. It was a true definition of faith as they decided, one by one, to join me in a quest where success was not guaranteed.

As any time management guru will tell you, it is wisest to focus clearly and wholly on one primary project at a time. That this kind of intense focus leads to better results and less overall stress. I agree—that's great advice. Rarely, however, do I follow it. Once we had this flywheel turning, it made sense to keep it turning as quickly as possible. Yes, it would be immensely helpful to have someone else on board to help run the program and yes, it would be fantastic to have funding for all of our projects, and yes, it was definitely too much for one person to take on, but the flywheel had to keep turning and I was hooked. I was hooked to the wheel itself and I was hooked to its success and I was hooked to the larger *why* that this program was about engaging students and developing a mindset that would lead to success. This program was not just a game changer, it was a world changer and it had too much potential to squander through whining.

That being said, I had little to nothing to offer the students who decided to join the teaching kitchen team. I had a budget of $150, I had a somewhat defective induction burner, I had a few pots and pans I had scrounged together, as well as a partially stained cutting board. Unlike the coffee bar where we had a set plan and strategy (along with a budget) to complete the build-out by the start of the school year and have the students running the business by September, this concept was far more ephemeral and the only deadline I had was the one I gave to David Eisenberg back at the Healthy Kitchens, Healthy Lives conference: eighteen months. Well, six of those months had already passed and this gave us one year. Twelve months. Twelve months to clear out the space, twelve months to raise funding, twelve months to build a program, twelve months to join the Teaching Kitchen Collaborative.

"Here's the deal," I began. "We've got an opportunity."

I proceeded to share my vision for the teaching kitchen. I spoke as if it already existed, as if the stainless-steel appliances were being unboxed as I spoke.

"And the best part," I said, "is we are going to build it here."

I gestured to the storage space around me as we stood in the middle of the unfinished space behind the greenhouse.

"Here?" one of the students asked. "As in, in this room?"

"Yes!" I said, excitement soaring through my voice. "This is our teaching kitchen. Can't you see it?"

I spread my arms so they could see what I saw. It seemed they couldn't. My years of teaching experience told me I was starting to lose some of them so I doubled down.

"Listen," I said, "I know what you're thinking. You're thinking this is some crazy dream, some unrealistic pitch that will never happen. You're thinking I'm going to get you to sign up for something that will never exist.

"Well listen and listen carefully—this *will* happen. We *will* have a teaching kitchen at this school and you, if you are brave enough and if you believe enough and if you are willing to put in the work and the time and the effort, you will see this happen during your time at the school.

"And look," I continued, "we have already started."

I gestured to the motley pile of defunct kitchen tools at my feet.

"You may look at this," I said, "you may see this pile and say, 'this will never happen' or 'it's not enough.' Well that's where you're wrong—this is more than just a chance to build something. This is an opportunity to change the entire way we think about education. This is an opportunity for you to do something no students have ever done before."

I paused and looked from student to student.

"I just need to know one thing—who's with me?"

The moment that every recruiter and inspirational speaker dreads was now upon me. I had thrown everything out and it was now up to them to take the bait and be willing to leap. And the uncomfortable silence seemed to last an eternity. It was broken, to my relief, by Max. Max, soon to be a senior, was an all-star football player who had known, since he was a young child, that he was called to be a chef. I first met Max when he was in eighth grade and I worked closely with him during the Food Symposium. Max was a hard worker and Max was a leader and if Max stepped up to join, it was guaranteed that others would follow.

"Mr. Carter," he said, "you had me at 'kitchen.'"

The other students surged forward, and it was in that moment that we all knew, collectively, that we were now doing the work of fulfilling dreams.

"Just one question," a student said, looking around the room. "I don't see any outlets. Do we even have electric?"

And just like that, our work began.

CHAPTER TEN

"The entrepreneurship program at CHCA was one of the best things I did while going to school there. It led me to passions I didn't even know I had and equipped me with tools and skills I can use for the rest of my life."

— Julianna, '23

In order to ensure that we would not make a mess of the greenhouse project, I spent a good deal of time in the summer of 2020 meeting with consultants and diving into my own horticulture education. Part of this effort was spent establishing the overarching *why* for the horticulture aspect of entrepreneurship. If our *why* was to run a business that makes money, then all the experts and consultants were suggesting that we create a sterile environment with little to no regular access, blowers at the door, and full plastic suits for the occasional visitor.

"Even the most well-intentioned person can accidentally cause harm in a greenhouse," one such consultant said. "We all have things on us without our knowing that can grow and fester in a setting like this. If you let visitors in, you are letting in bugs, and if you are letting in bugs, your work will never end."

With this ominous pronouncement in mind, I returned, somewhat defeated, to my makeshift office. Part of the vision of the space was to parade excited elementary students through and encourage them to plant, grow, and harvest. I had this vision of a third-grade student, surrounded by her peers, holding a head of lettuce as high as she could while the roots ran the length of her body and collected on the floor. The vision was not for a sterile, protected environment where hazmat suits were a requirement for entry. The vision was to be open to all and welcoming toward the spirit of entrepreneurship. How could people become inspired if they were forced to look in through a window?

In the end, although it meant we probably wouldn't have as amazing of a business as we could, we decided that having people in the space was more important. We prioritized education over sales. And, looking back, it was the perfect decision.

The rest of the summer was spent learning the ins and outs of horticulture. This meant that gardening became my new hobby. Not that this was rare—in the summer of 2020, it seemed that everyone who had access to dirt was learning how to garden. Now although I am not, by nature, a farmer, I had tended a home garden and over the years had started plenty of seeds and watered plants. But I was woefully underprepared to manage a greenhouse. And yet, rather than being overwhelming, this was invigorating. It was a challenge.

This is an important point to emphasize—the challenge. I've done a lot of reflecting on the development of the entrepreneurship program over the years and the primary driver of its growth has been challenge. The desire to push beyond what has been done, to try something new, to learn a new skill, to build something that has not been built before. It is the constant urge to create an environment where one is forced to sink or swim, the intoxicating pull of new obstacles and unchartered paths. I've learned a lot about myself and one of the primary lessons is this: I must always have a new challenge.

Early in my teaching career, I made a key decision. Having seen all too often the stereotypical teacher, thirty years into his career, who is phoning it in with time-worn lessons and little to no effort, I knew I had to take clear steps to avoid this fate. I made myself a deal: If I ever found that I was phoning it in or reusing something in the classroom simply because it was easy, if I discovered that I was no longer challenging myself to grow, then I would stop teaching. The art of teaching is far too valuable to be wasted on those who no longer care. Why would we ever entrust the learning of future generations to those who no longer learn themselves?

It is in the pursuit of the challenge that we learn our thresholds and it is in learning these thresholds that we can test our endurance by moving past them, further than we ever thought possible, into a space of victory and additional challenges. Each challenge, once met, should bring about another, larger challenge, and in this way, one is forced to continuously grow and get stronger or die trying. And I wasn't ready to die trying.

The challenge now was to become a proficient gardener—to become someone who could read soil conditions, coax seeds to sprout, nurture small plants to develop, and maintain the health of the garden. This was a challenge I was ready to throw everything I had into, and, thanks to COVID, time was abundant. I began reading Eliot Coleman and Wendell Berry. I watched a MasterClass on gardening, I scoured YouTube videos for tomato tips, I visited local farms to learn techniques, and I started thousands of seeds. I would be up at the greenhouse early in the morning to check on the seedlings and then would work through the day until late into the afternoon on clearing out the space and drawing up plans.

On many of these summer days, I recruited my own children, at the time nine and five years old, to help. For $7 an hour, they would organize seed packets, shovel dirt, and water seedlings. Day in and day out it was tending to the plants and then reading about how to tend to the plants and then tending to the plants some more. It was learning about pH and calcium, and it was understanding the use of neem oil and diatomaceous earth. And little by little, my proficiency grew, and little by little, the greenhouse came together.

Things were shifting into place and fast—once we received word that we would be conducting school in person (masked up and surrounded by plexiglass), it became go-time on all fronts. I was no longer officially an English teacher, but I had saddled myself with more than enough projects in overseeing not just the coffee bar but now a start-up venture in the greenhouse (to be called Eagle Farms) as well as a group dedicated to the building of a kitchen. While the greenhouse group would have plenty to do each class period (building the systems would take the bulk of the year), the culinary group not only had nothing to do but no space to do it in. Additionally, I had proposed a brand-new class for the year called Perspectives on Entrepreneurship. The class had been born out of the desire to create a certificate track for the program and to have a clear schedule of classes for students to take. Because the class was originally developed during COVID, it was designed to be remote and to use the podcasts (the ones already recorded and the ones that would be recorded—another one of my pressing tasks) as its curriculum. Since it was remote and could go in any class bell, it quickly expanded from a class of 24 students to a class of 130 students. This was all in addition to an agriculture and sustainability class I had inherited in taking on the greenhouse.

And so, with classes bursting at the seams, with uncertainty still in the air, and with dreams of incredible growth, we hit the ground running.

Which, in hindsight, looked a bit more like improvisation. A remote class based solely on podcasts? Let's do online Zoom discussions. An in-person class running a greenhouse business? Let's assemble raised beds and set up irrigation systems. A group of students scheduled for a seventh bell class called "Teaching Kitchen"? Let's—well, actually, that one was tough. And that meant it was time to get creative.

The space was certainly not functional—one primary outlet, unfinished walls, one utility sink, and some old science tables. The equipment was virtually nonexistent and the budget was already blown. And it was in this state that we learned perhaps the most valuable of lessons from the growth of the entrepreneurship program—things have far greater value when they've been grown from scratch, born out of hard work and determination. What we did have, and in abundance, was determination and once channeled, this force became truly powerful. We started with the equipment. Given that the kitchen was going to function as a lab and given that would be used by students, it made sense that a portion of the allotted auxiliary funding from the state could be used to purchase the necessities.

I reached out to the manager of our auxiliary funding and explained that we were building a kitchen lab that would function much like a science lab with regard to primary learnings and student engagement. I was requesting funding to purchase cutting boards, knives, induction burners, pots, and pans.

I was told no.

An outright, upfront refusal. I was told that the auxiliary funds could not be used for this sort of programming. Before I could counter, the line was disconnected.

Here we come to an important point in the development of our program: the refusal to listen to noes. Had I, after getting off the phone, faced the students and explained that we were not going to get any funding, I would be passing on this state of defeat. And I would certainly not be acting out the entrepreneurial mindset. The entrepreneurial mindset is chock-full of admirable qualities and chief among these is the refusal, within reason, to accept defeat.

It simply meant I had to go higher up the chain. So, I called the Ohio Department of Education.

The ODE can be a convoluted entity to penetrate with a single phone call, but after much bouncing around, I landed the ears of an individual specifically overseeing the allocation of state funding for independent schools. I made my case and I made it clear—we were teaching students fundamental skills directly linked to hands-on learning standards while using a space as a learning lab. I explained that this was as much an educational lab as anything done in science and that the students would be learning key competencies along the way.

And they said yes.

I will admit that I am someone who, at times, takes pleasure in the petty things and being able to call back the manager of our funding and explain that we would be purchasing cutting boards, knives, induction burners, pots and pans per a representative from the state department, well, that was one of those times.

Soon we had enough equipment for all twelve students. Armed with this confidence from such an early win, we set to work conducting class as if we were in a state-of-the-art commercial kitchen. We began with a knife skills tutorial and went through dicing, mincing, julienne, and brunoise. We then attempted to sauté the vegetables we had just cut, only to discover that our single outlet provided enough power for just one induction burner at a time. Rather than despair, we all simply huddled around the single burner (while social distancing and masking, of course) and worked in teams to cook the vegetables.

And just like that, a culinary program was born. It was born not in a ready-made, beautiful kitchen, but in the desire to learn to cook and to pursue it despite the obstacles. Perhaps even helped along by the obstacles. Because our electric was an issue, we began venturing outside, into the open air of our school grounds. We procured a grill, and were no longer tied to electric heat. We grilled everything from eggplant and poblano peppers to chicken and fish. One class, we even slapped a griddle on top of the grill and made pancakes. We had a teacher let us borrow his Ooni pizza oven and we started firing up pizzas during class. And we cooked—we cooked and we ate and we took as many pictures as were humanly possible.

And the word began to spread.

And as the word began to spread, the donors began to appear.

Imagine the experience of coming into an empty, unfinished space and seeing a group of students excited for a program that didn't even exist yet. Imagine seeing those students get pumped up about sourdough starter and the bread that comes from it. Imagine them blackening eggplants to make baba ghanoush. Imagine them growing tomatillos in the attached greenhouse only to blacken them over the flames of the grill before chopping them up and making a salsa verde.

It would be enough to cause anyone to open their checkbook. And they did.

In this way, we began to acquire the funds to build out the space as intended to create a beautiful, fully commercial teaching kitchen directly attached to the back of our four-thousand-square-foot greenhouse.

This is not to say that the funding came all at once. Instead, the plan for the kitchen grew based on the funding that came in. In other words, when we got our first $35,000, we designed a plan for a $35,000 kitchen. As that plan was coming together, we got another $10,000, and then decided we could do a $45,000 kitchen. In the first iteration, we were going to finish only half of the space leaving the other half an unfinished garage.

"Wait—so you're going to build this nice kitchen in half of the space and leave the other half looking like an unfinished room? Won't that kind of ruin the point?"

I had just finished giving a tour to our advancement director and sharing the dream of the kitchen. She was right and I knew it. We had to go big or go home. I called the contractor back and asked how much it would cost to finish the whole space and build a beautiful kitchen.

"You could probably do it for $150,000," he said.

I went to Dean and pled my case. I explained the situation and the desire to have an overall attractive space instead of a partially finished room. I even invited him to come teach a sample class in the existing space (which he did, to much applause from the students) so he could get a sense of our limitations. And, in the end, he directed me back to the school's teacher innovation fund. To say that the teacher innovation fund was instrumental in the growth of the entrepreneurship program is truly an understatement—we would not be where we are now without it. We received $60,000 in funding, which took us as close to our goal as we were able to get at the time—and close enough that we were able to start breaking ground.

CHAPTER ELEVEN

"Being a part of the entrepreneurship program completely changed the trajectory of what I wanted to do in college. It was the first platform I was given to be able to grow an entrepreneurial mindset and develop real world business skills. As I move forward as a dual entrepreneurship and finance major, I often reflect on the concepts and conversations that my time at CHCA brought to light."

— Bella, '22

In October 2020, I hit the wall. Hard.

For the first time in my career, I discovered two clear facts: Burnout is real and it is entirely preventable. Unfortunately, I discovered the second fact after I discovered the first one.

The heavily weighted reality of everything I was trying to accomplish in a program run by one person confronted me head-on and knocked the wind out of me. On the surface, everything seemed fine—the kitchen was under construction, the greenhouse was thriving, the coffee bar was moving full steam ahead, the perspectives class was getting solid reviews, and student interest was high. Just below the surface, however, not everything was fine.

I would arrive at the greenhouse early in the morning, drop my bag in the small area of the storage space not roped off with caution tape, and sit down in a folding chair positioned by a rickety table to check my email. Immediately, I would be hit by a range of symptoms including fatigue, stress, exhaustion, irritability, lack of interest, and a sense of being overwhelmed.

The following thoughts would invade my thinking:

"The kitchen will never be built."

"Even if it is built, students will not want to take classes out here."

"I won't be able to raise the money."

"The greenhouse will be overtaken by bugs."

"I'll get COVID and be quarantined for weeks and everything will fall apart."

Once I worked through these thoughts, new ones would take their place:

"What's the point, anyway?"

"Does anyone even care that I'm doing all of this?"

"Is it worth the struggle? Should I just not even try?"

For the duration of my career up to this point, I'd been able to keep feelings like this at bay. I believed in my programming and had developed the necessary time management skills to find true balance in life. And yet, through my excitement for the program and its potential, I had allowed my "yes mindset" to take on too much—for one person, at least. There were only two options I could see: Either slow down and give something up, or figure out a way to grow the team. Slowing down seemed wrong on every level—it was an admission of defeat and there was nothing I was willing to let fall through the cracks. This meant the only option was to hire someone, and this now became my driving ambition.

As anyone in administration knows, it is no small task to add a new employee payroll to the overall budget once the school year is underway—decisions like this are made months in advance and finalized well before the end of the previous school year. And yet, it seemed to be my only option. I had discovered, to my surprise, that I had limits. I actually *could not* do it all myself. But, at the same time, it all had to be done.

I made a list of my current responsibilities:

1. Directly overseeing the 27 students working and operating the coffee bar
2. Teaching 130 students in the online perspectives on entrepreneurship course
3. Maintaining a podcast with regular guests and extensive audio editing
4. Teaching an agriculture and sustainability course with 12 students
5. Overseeing a 4,000-square-foot greenhouse and its production schedule
6. Working with elementary students in the outdoor raised-bed garden area
7. Attempting to resurrect and beautify a defunct vineyard on the campus
8. Working with students to launch a brand-new business selling the greenhouse produce through an e-commerce platform

9. Meeting with contractors to build a kitchen on an incredibly tight budget
10. Teaching a makeshift culinary class to the students working on the kitchen project
11. Writing the curriculum for the overall program in order to create a certificate track

Clearly, it was time for a change.

I had established a regular meeting schedule with our head of school, Randy Brunk. Over the last few years of the program's development, I had come to have more and more interaction with Randy and had seen him oversee a capital campaign as well as work individually with donors (he helped facilitate the first $50,000 gift to the program).

"So how are *you* doing?" he asked, after I had finished peppering him with questions about systems and structures and program development.

"I'm OK," I said. "The work is energizing."

"I mean how are *you* doing?"

I hesitated. Then decided to tell the truth.

"Stressed, actually," I said. "Lots and lots of stress."

I proceeded to explain all the various projects currently underway that I was overseeing (and doing myself). I was also quick to point out that no one—not him, not Dean, not any board member—had requested that I take all this on. All of these projects I had taken on myself in an attempt to grow the best entrepreneurship program in the world.

"So why do you suppose you are doing all of these things?" Randy asked. "Are there any of them you can let go of?"

"Most likely," I said, "but this program is far too exciting for me to slow down. I know some of these things may not be the things that will build it, but I can't risk being the lid on growth." I had just reread John Maxwell's Law of the Lid and was intensely conscious of my own shortcomings being a bottleneck to progress.

"Are there any of these things you can have someone help you with?" he asked.

"I would love help," I said, "but the truth is, it would require hiring someone. Everything that we're building here, everything that is underway, is so new and specific that it would need to be someone from the outside coming in and joining this as if it's a start-up. And I highly doubt you'll let me hire a new full-time person at this point."

Randy sat back and looked around the space. The greenhouse was flourishing with trellised cucumbers reaching up to the ceiling and tower gardens bursting with green. The space where we were sitting was a construction zone with drywall studs lining the wall and several large appliances wrapped in drop cloths. Depending on one's perspective, it either looked full of promise and potential or an absolute disaster.

"There is one idea that might be of interest," I said, wanting to take advantage of this pause.

Randy turned to look at me, interest creeping over his face.

"I'm listening," he said.

"The truth is," I said, "I need help. Lots of help. I'm spinning my wheels and have far too many projects going on simultaneously but I'm also unwilling to give any of them up as the program's growth is too important. I need someone else on my team."

I paused and Randy remained silent.

"I also understand," I continued, "that the school can't realistically hire someone this far into the year given the stated overall budget."

"It would be complicated," Randy said. "It would involve the board and would be a process."

"And I don't feel we can wait for that," I said. "So, I have a proposal to pay for the salary of the new hire."

I began to break down all the financials of the program, starting with the coffee bar. Although COVID had shut us down last spring, the coffee bar was back up and running full steam (plexiglass and all) and was poised to reach gross revenues of $40,000 this school year. Not only that, but the greenhouse e-commerce start-up, Eagle Farms, had kicked off with a bang and was pulling in monthly gross revenues of close to $3,000.

"What if," I said, "we hire someone to help, and the program pays the salary."

I paused and waited.

"That definitely changes things," Randy said.

"Look, when this is built," I said, gesturing to the space around us, "this will give opportunity and space for multiple streams of revenue, which will more than cover the salary of the new hire. In other words—suppose we treated this program like a business, like an actual entrepreneurship venture and we started paying our own way."

The more I talked, the more Randy's composure changed and by the end of the conversation, he had agreed to allow a new, full-time hire into the program with the understanding that the salary would be covered by the program revenue. I was sent to the business office to iron out the details and, similar to the deal with the coffee bar loan, I was given a one-year up-front loan for the salary with a payback plan going into effect the following school year.

Within a week, I had a job description on the school's website and was fielding applications. The job focused primarily on managing the school's greenhouse—a blend of horticulture, agriculture, teaching, and organizing. And among the pile of applications, one name stood out: Turner Shrout. Turner had been my English student for tenth and twelfth grade and had even participated in the debate team I was overseeing. The final piece that seemed to immediately seal the deal was the fact that Turner was part of the group of students who originally launched the coffee bar—a true full-circle moment. Having just graduated from college, Turner was looking for an opportunity just as this job opening became available.

During the interview process, I explained that, on some level, I had no idea what this job would look like in the coming months and that it would involve attempting to control the chaos of growth the program was experiencing. I wanted to make sure Turner was OK with that environment and was incredibly pleased when she came on board. Now there were two people working toward the overarching goal of program growth. Now there were two people to manage the ever-expanding list of responsibilities.

What I didn't account for, in my exuberance to bring someone else on board, was how to begin creating a team culture in the program. Up to this point, I had been running solo, lone wolf style, fighting for scraps and building dreams on nothing but air and small bits of funding. This mentality, so common in entrepreneurship, does not necessarily lead to a strong team culture. While Turner was great about coming into this burgeoning environment, it is safe to say that I was far from the ideal team leader. I had gone fourteen years in my career before having a direct report and now that I had one, I had no idea how to lead. So I did what came naturally—shared the vision, explained the dream, and gave over as much responsibility as felt necessary.

And, despite a few bumps in the road, the program grew.

CHAPTER TWELVE

"The CHCA entrepreneurship program has provided me with an experience that is truly one of a kind. The lessons and confidence I learned have empowered me to meet the world's challenges head on."

— Ben, '23

While having doubled the size of our leadership team certainly helped, it also brought us back face-to-face with several seemingly insurmountable obstacles. The biggest one was the kitchen. We had started down the route of construction and had created three phases that allowed us to dive into the project despite not having all the funding in place. Worst-case scenario, the first two phases would give us a workable space even if the remainder was left unfinished. So funding was still a primary obstacle—we were short on our total project cost by around $10,000. Space was now a second obstacle—in order to start the kitchen build-out, we had to jump through numerous hoops with the contractors and vacate the space for several months. This was especially problematic as the space under construction was functioning as my classroom for the twelve culinary students and now we were not only without a kitchen but even without a base of operations.

It was in this desperate situation that an unlikely, unassuming hero presented itself. And it was unlikely and unassuming because it was covered in sauce and cheese. The concept of creating a business around selling pizzas was born out of a conversation we had as a group just after receiving word that we would be unable to continue to meet in the unfinished space as it was officially under construction.

"So what do we do now?" one of the students asked.

"I'm at a bit of a loss," I said, looking around at the group. "There's not much we can do until our space is finished, and that is likely to take quite some time. I'm hoping it will be done by the end of the school year, but I'm not sure."

I looked around the space, and, after surveying the draping caution tape and piles of construction materials, began to readjust mid-thought.

"Perhaps we might have to have class virtually for a while."

A collective groan ensued from the students.

"A virtual culinary class? That's not what we signed up for."

"Yeah, it was better when we at least had a space where we could do *some* cooking. Now we aren't even allowed in this room!"

The students were referring to the sign now posted explaining that, due to the start of construction, classes were no longer permitted to meet.

"We can keep grilling and stuff like that," someone offered. "There's still outside spaces."

"We've done all that," another said, "and it's getting old. Not to mention cold. And rainy."

Cincinnati weather is famous for its unpredictability and this season was especially unpredictable, which made it difficult to plan for any outside culinary ventures.

"Don't we still need $10,000 for the kitchen?" someone asked. "Like we don't even have all the money we need to finish the project?"

"Yes," I said, "but you don't need to worry about that—I'll keep searching for a donor. I'm confident we will get the funds to finish the project."

"Even then," someone added, "it still will be forever until we can meet again."

"Unless we did something creative," said a voice from the back.

We all turned to see Max, dressed in his football jersey and carrying a jug of water. Max's innate culinary skills coupled with the fact that he was a senior and a football player gave him a sense of gravitas. Everyone grew silent.

"What did you have in mind?" someone finally asked, breaking the spell.

"This," said Max, pointing to the corner of the space. "I have this in mind."

The entire group looked from Max to the corner of the room and then back to Max.

"I'm confused," a few of the students said.

Max walked over to where he was pointing and lifted an object into the air.

"The Ooni pizza oven!" a student cried out. "I forgot we had that!"

We still had the personal wood-fired pizza maker that had been loaned to us from a teacher at the school. This had made for several exciting classes as students experimented with a few different dough types ultimately landing on their preferred ratio of flour to water. After that, the Ooni had sat, unused, and had been moved to the side of the room at the start of construction.

"So your idea is we make pizzas?" a student said, turning to Max.

"That's only half my idea," Max said. "My main idea is that we sell them—the pizzas, I mean. Let's start a business selling wood-fired pizzas."

"Like to other students?" someone asked.

"When, after school?" another person asked.

"Would anyone buy them?" yet another asked.

Suddenly, and without missing a beat, the class became abuzz with excitement and began talking hurriedly.

"That's it—we can make them during our bell and then we can sell them after school."

"And we can even sell them at events like plays and games and stuff."

"They *are* delicious."

"Truth—I mean, I'd buy them."

It was decided unanimously that our class, on hold due to construction, would pivot (a term we had become quite familiar with during this COVID stretch) to create a brand-new business that would both fill our class time and (hopefully) create revenue for our construction project. With renewed energy, our group jumped into the wood-fired pizza business with gusto. They started building interest by cooking up a number of pizzas during class and then handing out free slices to students in the building. A small group of them began to survey their fellow students regarding pizza preferences, recommended pricing, and consumer interest. Still others experimented with various toppings until arriving at the margherita. It was right about this time that the tomatoes in the greenhouse had begun to ripen, and we set up a table outside the greenhouse with a cutting board, a knife, and an induction burner to make our own pizza sauce.

Meanwhile, we did some research and landed on the specialty field of certified Neapolitan pizzas, which turned into a fascinating study that ultimately led us to a company that imported traditional Italian pizza ovens into the United States. Using a special Saputo stone, these ovens could get up to 900 degrees without burning the pizza and three pizzas could be cooked at one time (with an average cook time of two minutes). Using the simplest and freshest of ingredients, a pizza perfect in crust and flavor could be created. And although a price can never be placed on perfection, we arrived, after much deliberation, market research, and itemized pricing, at a starting point of $8 for a cheese pizza.

The work continued—day after day, class after class, we cranked out pizzas to determine exact timing, perfect amount of ingredients, and specific methods for handling a rush of orders. We practiced making three pizzas at once and we practiced spacing out our orders. We troubleshooted for potentially difficult customers and worst-case scenarios. We went over every specific role in finite details, even drawing up a map of where everyone would stand. We did several sample run-throughs where we pretended the orders were coming in, setting up a point-of-sale system and communicating to the back of house. We practiced dealing with frustrating order modifications, and we developed a quality control system. Finally, after a month and a half of work, Eagle Pizza, Co. was ready to open for business.

And open we did—just forty-five days after the initial conversation, our first customers began lining up. And then more. And then more. Word had gotten out and two things began to happen simultaneously—first, students began to walk through the building holding a pizza box emblazoned with "Eagle Pizza, Co.," which immediately attracted questions and attention. Second, the pizza oven, which, despite its large size, had two wheels on the back of it making it somewhat mobile, had been wheeled to the primary doors of the school so that everyone entering and exiting at the end of the day was forced to walk by. Imagine walking out of the school and seeing a blazing fire in a wood oven while a group of students were slinging pizzas in and out and into boxes for hungry customers. No additional marketing was necessary.

The first day we were open from 3 p.m. until 4:30 p.m. and we sold over eighty pizzas. The only reason we didn't sell more is because we sold out—and brought in close to $800 in gross revenue. Keep in mind that The Leaning Eagle, in its current iteration, was bringing in around $200 in gross revenue each day from eight hours of operation, so to quadruple that in an hour and a half definitely attracted some notice. Also consider that the profit margin (which the students meticulously calculated in the days leading up to our grand opening) hovered around 70 percent, making the total profit close to $560. In short, we were in business, and loving every bit of it. The grand opening had the same intoxicating excitement that the opening of the coffee bar had brought five years earlier.

Each Friday for the rest of the year, we rolled the pizza oven to the front of the school and cooked as many pizzas as possible for the short time after school as students left and headed to their afternoon activities. And each Friday, we slowly increased the number of pizzas available until we maxed out at 120 (which brought in over $1,000 in gross revenue). The business had drawn enough attention that teachers and parents from other buildings were coming over to order, and we even had a few community members begin lining up outside on Fridays. Some of our especially gritty students even began canvasing local neighborhoods and businesses and, as I later found out, started promising delivery.

As the director of entrepreneurship, one wears many hats. One of these hats, it turns out, is pizza delivery guy. Because I was uncomfortable sending any of our underclassmen out for deliveries and because the upperclassmen were tied up making pizzas, I became the default delivery person. This meant backing my car up to the pizza station, loading it up for several orders, and taking off. But the truth is, I was having a blast—seeing the students working together was like watching a symphony in action. They moved with a rhythm all their own, and their ownership over the concept was palpable.

Over the following months, Eagle Pizza, Co. established itself as the most profitable business in the program. The students began to do special events and add specialty pizzas, and they even created an online ordering system to enable preorders, thus averting the problem of running out of product before their regular customers could make it to their stand. And the profits came in—by the end of the school year, the students had paid off the pizza oven and additional equipment and had begun contributing directly to the kitchen project. But more importantly, they had engaged in the experience in a powerful way and thereby had learned a set of valuable skills that cannot be taught in a traditional classroom.

And this is perhaps the biggest takeaway and the reason I say that this program is so important—these students are learning not just how to be entrepreneurs, but how to *think* like entrepreneurs. They are not just problem-solving, they are problem-solving in the real world. They are not just working on a team, they are *relying* on a team. They are not just seeking opportunities, they are *chasing down* opportunities. They are embodying what is meant by innovative education and they are preparing themselves for success in an ever-changing world. And as someone who gets to witness this on a daily basis, it is nothing short of inspiring.

CHAPTER THIRTEEN

"The entrepreneurship program impacted me to think outside of the box and collaborate in a positive way with my peers. It also inspired me to chase a degree in entrepreneurship at the university level because of how much I enjoyed seeing our success which came through failures grew our own start-up business while in high school."

— Victory, '22

I'd be fooling myself if I said these student-run businesses would have been successful simply because of a strategically assembled team. Every successful business that has come out of our program has been successful because it has been championed by a student leader. Over the years, as the businesses get handed down, new champions step up to take the place of the original, but the key to success is in the passion, dedication, and, ultimately, work ethic of the student driving the work. And in the case of Eagle Pizza, Co., that person was Max.

This is not to say that the rest of the team didn't pull their weight—to the contrary, they worked harder than I've ever seen a team of high schoolers work. They showed up early and they stayed late, they cleaned dishes, and they designed systems. They truly played the part of a high-functioning group, but they had a clear leader in the senior athlete whose happy space is the kitchen.

I first met Max when his older brother, one of my English students, dragged him into class to meet me.

"Mr. Carter," Ben said, holding a shorter version of himself by the collar. "This is Max. Max, say hi to Mr. Carter."

"Hi," Max said, looking down.

"Hi, Max," I said. "To what do I owe this pleasure."

"Well, I know how much you like talking about food," Ben said, "and my brother is obsessed with it. He's going to be a chef someday."

"Is that so?" I said, looking at Max.

"Yes, sir," he said, making eye contact with me. "I am."

That moment ingrained itself in my memory not only as the first time I met Max but as a sense of awe at the ability of a thirteen-year-old to know, definitively, his life calling. Over the next several years, I came to know Max more and more and never once did I, or anyone else, question that he knew, beyond a shadow of a doubt, what he was going to pursue for the rest of his life.

In a program where we emphasize, at all levels in and all circumstances, the importance of growth mindset, grit, redefining failure, and opportunity seeking, there are some students, rare though they may be, who come in as shining beacons of these qualities. There are some students who naturally radiate the entrepreneurial mindset in all areas. And Max was one of these students. Now before you assume that Max was a superstar in all areas, please understand that he did not stand out as a stellar student. Yes, he completed his work, and yes, he did what was required, but having had Max in an honors English class, I can certainly say that he did not get the highest grades in the class (although he did quite well).

And this is important—so often our academic programming focuses on the top-scoring students who can easily ace tests and who have intuitive knowledge of how to get perfect grades. This is not the case with entrepreneurship. Entrepreneurship, as an academic program, reaches all learners. I think back to Jake, who oversaw the merger of the coffee bar and the smoothie bar. Jake pushed against every traditional assessment in the classroom—he rarely turned in papers, he was easily distracted, and often distracted others. He was not what most teachers would call a stellar student. If asked, he would most likely have said that he hated every bit of every classroom at the school.

Yet when managing the coffee bar, Jake was in his element. He grew several inches taller in his pride and self-confidence, he discovered a hidden skill set around systems and organization, and he took the program to a new level. Jake thrived. And as a result, the program thrived. And this is not an isolated case—over the last ten years, this has happened again and again. All the while, however, traditionally successful students have also thrived. Allie, our original COO of the coffee bar, was in every respect a perfect student. Straight As and polished work, she was the darling of the classroom teacher. But she also completely revolutionized the coffee bar and brought a level of excellence to it during her tenure. And both Jake and Allie still stop by, years later, to check on its progress (and to function as secret shoppers).

Max had this same drive and ability. And he knew what he wanted. When Max's friends were hanging out after school and doing all the typical things that high schoolers do, Max was searching for a job at a restaurant. He was hired as a busboy at a fancy, local steakhouse, and day after day, he wiped tables and cleaned up after patrons while ignoring the pleas from his friends to quit and hang out with them. Over his high school years, he worked his way up to the line and began preparing food. By the time Max was engaged in starting Eagle Pizza, Co., he had become indispensable to the restaurant and had been promoted to sous chef. The owner was even pleading with him to come work full-time after high school.

But Max knew what he wanted, and he knew that the path to get there was through the CIA. The Culinary Institute of America, whose Hyde Park, New York, campus is famous among chefs, is the shining star of the culinary school world, and Max was determined to get a spot in the upcoming freshman class. So, he focused on it. Day in and day out, he honed his skills, and he worked his job, and he somehow managed to also do his coursework and thrive in sports. When the time came to write his college essay, he was able to tell his journey to help build a teaching kitchen at his school—a journey that included starting a brand-new business. And not many applicants were able to say all of that.

We celebrated the day Max got his acceptance letter—the whole class cheered, and we could tell we were witnessing a dream come true. Later, when I asked him how many other schools he had applied to, he answered, "Just the one. And that's all I needed." Max's story does reflect many aspects of what we try to teach regarding the entrepreneurial mindset, but the wonderful thing about his story is that it didn't stop there. Max continued to use his growth mindset, his grit, his ability to redefine failure, and his sense of opportunity seeking to make a name for himself in his freshman class at the CIA.

There is something intoxicating about a person who has become wholly immersed in his element and this is what the culinary instructors discovered about Max. Max is a driven individual, and you can't tell a driven individual to slow down. Perhaps the most striking example of his mindset came toward the end of his freshman year. All the first-year culinary students at the CIA seek internships for the summer in restaurants around the world, and the better the restaurant, the more sought-after the position.

This is why many of the students apply at Alinea in Chicago. Alinea opened in 2005 and by 2010, it had three stars from the Michelin Guide, and by 2016 chef and owner Grant Achatz was featured on the Netflix show *Chef's Table*. In addition to constantly ranking as one of the top restaurants in the world, it is a mecca for foodies and for aspiring chefs. Thus, the large number of applications from CIA hopeful students for only a few coveted internship spots. The process is straightforward: a student sends in an application and gets a response saying that in order to be considered, they have to schedule a time in the coming months to "stage," which essentially means working for free for a short period of time to demonstrate skills and kitchen confidence.

The typical reaction of the CIA student, upon receiving this response, is to check the calendar, then call the parents, then go about the rest of the day while deciding when would be best to schedule a visit to the restaurant. This, however, was not Max's response. Max, long a student at the school of Caerus, got the response from the restaurant, and saw it for the opportunity it was. He dropped his pen, closed his laptop, grabbed his keys, and dashed to his car. He pulled out his phone and entered the restaurant's address (a twelve-hour drive) and he took off, stopping only to fill up with gas.

Max arrived at Alinea a few hours before service. He went straight to the door and knocked. *As an aside, isn't this what we want for all of our students? To head straight to the door and knock? To knock with expectation, to know that they will be welcomed in, granted a seat at the table? Yet so often, we fail to give them the tools and the mindset to do this for themselves.*

Max knocked.

And the door opened.

And when a man decked in a full chef coat stepped down to greet him, Max held out his hand and said simply, "My name is Max and I'm going to be your next intern." And just like that (along with a few days of proving himself in the kitchen), Max landed an internship at one of the finest restaurants in the world.

He called me a few days later to tell me the story and when I got off the phone with him, I felt pure, unadulterated joy flood my body. Not pride or a sense of ownership, but joy. Max had chased down opportunity, grabbed it by the hair, and seized it for all its possibility. And he was triumphant. And this brings out an important point—we all want our students as well our own children to find happiness. We say this over and over and over: "Chase your dreams and become happy," but often we misguide them in the method of this. Happiness is fleeting, a momentary emotion whose transient nature often eludes us. And thus, the quest for happiness has misled many a young person who believes that, once in the perfect job or perfect situation, nothing will be difficult or challenging.

This is a dangerous belief—Max was not chasing happiness. Max was chasing opportunity. The happiness comes from the seizing of the opportunity and lasts just long enough to enable us to set the next goal, an essential step in prolonging the happiness. Max's long hours that summer, spent tediously chopping onions, mincing garlic, and doing menial kitchen tasks, cannot be described as happy. Nor can it be said he was happy when his high school friends, drifting listlessly throughout the summer, would text to hang out and he had to say no. Max was not chasing an ephemeral emotion—he was chasing a dream.

I recently took my wife to our favorite restaurant in Cincinnati. Driven by the personality of the owner and operator, this restaurant takes fine dining to the next level, fueled by a commitment to create unforgettable moments—a philosophy embedded in every aspect of the dining experience. People are expecting good service? Give them amazing service they will never forget. People are expecting delicious food? Make the food so good that every bite is a technicolor dream. And the restaurant team delivers. Toward the end of our dinner, the chef came to our table and the talk turned to the life of a chef.

"Some people will come to me," he said, "and they will say, 'I think I want to become a chef' and I immediately say 'NO!'"

When the chef talks, his arms become his punctuation marks, emphasizing his points in direct relation to the tenor of his voice.

"NO!" he said again. "Do not become a chef. Why not? Because you said, 'I think.' 'I think I want to become a chef.'"

He paused.

"It's like this," he continued. "You either know or you don't. This is not the life for someone who just thinks, 'Oh, maybe I will.' You have to commit. It's a life of brutality over and over. It's wonderful, yes, but it's only for the committed."

The chef moved on to greet other people, but his words stayed with me long past that night. As someone who has always been drawn to the food industry and specifically fine dining, I can begin to grasp what he is describing and think of it as what we often refer to as "a calling." Something that promises not happiness, not comfort, not a life of ease, but rather a life of drive and passion and purpose that fuels the everyday activities into the realization that the *why* is more important than the individual action

This can be the life of the chef and it can be the life of the teacher and it can be the life of the doctor, the lawyer, the office worker, the administrative assistant, the line worker, the cashier, the accountant, and the electrician. This can be the life of the entrepreneur. The difference between a job and a calling is in the understanding of the *why*, and the acceptance of the grind and occasional brutality because of the connection to the higher purpose.

And nowhere is this more apparent than in the culinary world. Looking back, it is easy to connect the dots between the growth of the entrepreneurship program and the connection to culinary studies, but at the time, there was something more subtle, more subconscious working in the background to bring these concepts together. Perhaps somewhere, deeply ingrained in the core psyche of the entrepreneurial mindset there exists a desire to seek out the problem-solving occupations that require hard work and dedication above all else. Who, other than someone operating with an entrepreneurial mindset, would seek out a life of brutality simply for a few shots of glory and triumph? Who other than someone operating with core values of growth mindset, grit, redefining failure, and opportunity seeking would want to be a chef?

Max worked harder that summer than he had ever worked in his life, and he did this day after day after day. He moved up the ranks and proved himself to be more than just an intern—he became invaluable. At the end of the summer, he was offered a full-time job. When he turned it down to return to culinary school to complete his degree, he was told that the job would be waiting for him when he graduated. As I write these words, Max has now graduated from the Culinary Institute of America and has started his full-time career at Alinea.

Without getting too ahead of the story, allow me to say that now, when students come into our teaching kitchen and they are introduced to the strict procedures and systems that guide all of our actions, when they have to scrub dishes and clean counters, and when they have to clean up after themselves, that what they are really learning, on a deeper level, is how to embrace a calling. We are not in the business of creating or manifesting happiness. We are in the business of mindset and that mindset does not guarantee a life of ease, but it does ultimately help in pursuing a life of meaning.

CHAPTER FOURTEEN

"The entrepreneurship program allowed me to be heavily involved in a business setting long before the average teen. I developed great mental, educational, and professional habits as the result of participating in an actual business. This program encouraged and inspired me to further my study at the Kelley School of Business."

— Ava, '23

When we talk about giving students "real-world experience," the learning is delivered in unexpected ways. For instance, rather than explain to students how frustrating it can be to work with a contractor or how delays and construction projects go hand in hand, you could just have them take part in the process of building a teaching kitchen. If you want to teach them about the ridiculous nature of government bureaucracy, for instance, just have them spend five minutes in the presence of a building inspector. These are the life lessons that cannot be taught in a traditional classroom and, once learned, are never forgotten.

The students in the first culinary class that designed and worked to build the teaching kitchen did not, in the course of their school year, get to see the kitchen built. Three graduating seniors in the group were never able to cook in the finished space. And that was unfortunate, but it was also a lesson in realism—sometimes it takes a bit longer for dreams to come true. And when they do come true, they are often all the sweeter for it. Such as when, in the summer of 2023, in between his graduation at the Culinary Institute of America and the start of his work at Alinea, Max Vonderhaar returned to the finished teaching kitchen space and conducted a sold-out cooking class which featured, among other delights, the best duck I've had in my life. Assisting him in the class was a student who a high school senior fresh off of graduation who had, while he was a student, operated the wood-fired pizza business Max helped start. There's a certain power to stories that come full circle.

As the finishing touches were coming together for the kitchen, the work to put together proposed courses for the following year began. The space was designed to have a dual purpose, like the greenhouse, that would serve both educational needs and entrepreneurship opportunities. This led to the creation of a foundations-level culinary class open to all grades as well as leaving several bells open for what we were now calling the "entrepreneurship internship course." Over the years, the class title for the students enrolled in managing the coffee bar went through multiple iterations but now that there were multiple businesses involved, including Eagle Farms and Eagle Pizza, Co., it made sense to refer to all of them collectively as the entrepreneurship internships. This way, students could sign up for the same "experience" though it may be at one of three or four businesses. It would also leave room for the development of a new business the following year, possibly a bakery or other kitchen-themed project. After all, we now had the space.

What we didn't have was the chef.

In a recent development, Dean had moved to assistant head of school and Heather Wilkowski was now the principal of the upper school. A huge fan of the entrepreneurship program as her oldest son had gone through it recently, Heather truly understood the possibilities at play.

"Heather," I said, as I started off the meeting I had called to discuss the future plans of the kitchen, "I want you to imagine a space where students can take a course to learn culinary skills in a fully commercial kitchen. Picture them sauteing, grilling, braising, and roasting. Imagine them embracing the entrepreneurial mindset while understanding not only where their food comes from but how to turn it into delicious meals. Think of the empowerment."

Heather smiled and continued to listen. Like Dean, she knew a large request was coming.

"Which brings me to my ask—"

Over the years I had, as you well know by now, asked for many things. While I didn't always get a yes, I usually got a response that was, in hindsight, fair. Sometimes this answer was "no" or "not yet" or "get creative with it." And as frustrating as those answers were, they did often lead to better results.

This time, however, I wanted a yes.

"We need a full-time chef."

She was silent.

"On staff," I continued, "like a faculty member. A teacher-chef. To have a full load of classes."

She finally spoke.

"Do you have enough students to justify hiring a full-time chef?" she asked.

I explained that we would be offering three culinary foundations classes each semester and that each class would max out at twelve students. The twelve-to-one ratio was due to one instructor overseeing sharp knives, gas burners, and food processors. The other two classes, which would then max out a five bell full-time load, would be entrepreneurship ventures like The Leaning Eagle.

"It sounds to me like you need about sixty total students for the culinary class," she said. "I tell you what: you get sixty students to sign up and we'll hire a chef."

"Seriously?" I asked incredulously. I had prepared for more debate, for presentation of data, and for the start of a long, drawn-out discussion. Instead, she had given a clear benchmark.

"Seriously," she said.

I left Heather's office and got straight to work. I began by emailing each teacher in the school and asking if I could have three minutes from their homeroom class to describe an exciting new program at the school. One by one, I went around and made the pitch of my life.

"I want you to consider an experience unlike anything you've had in high school so far," I began before painting a picture of what the elective experience would be like.

"Imagine the smells and the tastes and the flavors," I continued, shamelessly plugging the program for all it was worth. I pitched the future class with fervor and passion and belief.

And the students signed up. And signed up. And signed up.

In the end, we had 170 students sign up for class that, over the course of the year, only had spots for 72. This meant that close to 100 students would not get a spot and this, then, caused a whole other slew of problems. The next week I found myself back in Heather's office.

"What do I do with the one hundred students that don't have a spot?" she asked. "What do I tell the parents? Is there any way to extend the space, or add another teacher?"

I sat back and smiled. Not to offend her, but at the irony of the situation. Here I was, trying to troubleshoot an abundance of interest. We had sought sixty-five and had come back with almost three times that number. We had proven that the model worked and that students wanted the experience.

We had found success before we even started.

"So I assume I can hire a chef?" I asked.

"Yes," she said, and quickly added, "and maybe two."

In the end, we settled for one.

It turns out that it is a dramatically different experience hiring for a chef educator than a typical teaching position. First, it was clear that we were looking for someone with culinary experience and second it was clear that we were looking for someone with teaching experience. And the hope was that they were accomplished at both. And then the hope is that they are good with students. And finally, the hope is that the students will like the teacher and enjoy the class. Of course, the hope is also that they will sign the contract once they see the salary.

Our chef instructor was hired in May as the finishing touches were being put on the teaching kitchen and by August 2021, when we held our grand opening, she was charged with hitting the ground running by starting up a brand-new culinary program. I shared with her my goal of joining the Teaching Kitchen Collaborative and therefore my commitment to healthy, nutritious food, and then she shared her own personal food journey with me. As we talked, it became obvious that she was passionate about cuisine from around the world and had spent time living in several different countries. The more she shared, the more she lit up when talking about international cuisine.

"It sounds to me like you are wanting to teach an international food course," I said.

"Oh, could I?" she asked, eyes wide with anticipation. "I would love that."

"Sure," I said. "I want you to teach what you love; that is how we get the students to love it."

"What would that kind of course look like? Could I plan it with cuisine from around the world?"

Over the next few hours, we mapped out an entire semester class that started in Latin America before venturing into Europe to visit Italy and France and Germany before heading to the Middle East and finally into Asia. And the end of the semester, the students would return to the United States and look at the true melting pot nature of cuisine. And all while having a class in the brand-new teaching kitchen. To top it off, they would engage in a *Chopped*-style competition in lieu of a final exam.

The course looked amazing, and the new kitchen looked spectacular, and all of this made me feel that we were ready for the next step. And that next step was to reach back out to David Eisenberg.

"Hi Dr. Eisenberg," I typed into the email, "we met at the 2020 Healthy Kitchens, Healthy Lives Conference." I continued to type, explaining our journey toward creating a teaching kitchen with the intent of becoming the first K–12 school in the world to join the collaborative. I shared about the number of interested students and about the hiring of a full-time chef. I explained our international cuisine course as culinary foundations and I ended the email with a series of attached pictures showing the space and the official grand opening. In a PS at the very bottom, I explained that it was almost eighteen months to the day since we last communicated.

The email was sent and then the waiting began. But the waiting did not last for long—my phone rang with an unknown number, and I answered it to hear the voice of David Eisenberg himself.

"Stephen, a hearty congratulations," he said. "I'm so thrilled for you."

"Thank you, sir, it's an honor just to speak with you," I said, not a little starstruck. It's worth pointing out that Dr. David Eisenberg, for all his accomplishments and accolades, is one of the most kind, humble and caring people I've ever met. When he talks to you, he *talks* to you. He is present and his compassion flows through his words. David has the eyes of someone who sees through to one's inner soul and affirms the nature of one's presence. He is simply a wonderful man.

He explained that although I was a little behind on the timing for the current year's openings, and that he was entirely shocked we had moved this quickly, there was still enough opportunity to move forward for this year. After hanging up, I immediately began filling out our application and submitting the appropriate paperwork. The whirlwind of the start of a new year with new classes and new programming all faded as I found a single-minded focus and pursuit of one goal and one goal only—*we were going to join the Teaching Kitchen Collaborative.*

And join we did. David informed us that we would become certified members just a few months later in early 2022. Which meant that Cincinnati Hills Christian Academy would officially become the first K–12 school to join the collaborative between Harvard University's T. H. Chan School of Public Health and the Culinary Institute of America. And to top it off, we would be included with our own page on the website.

My phone rang later that day.

"Stephen?" a familiar voice said.

"Dr. Eisenberg!" I said with a bit too much excitement.

"Call me David," he said. "I want to congratulate you and tell you how glad I am that you are part of this. And how excited I am that you will be leading the charge into getting teaching kitchens into every school across the United States."

He paused while I let this sink in. This was clearly bigger than a single kitchen in a single school.

"You see, Stephen," he said, "you may not know this yet, but this is like a wildfire. This will surge. The excitement and the energy from your students will boil over and other schools will follow in your wake."

"Yes, sir," I said, "however we can help, we are on board."

"Stephen," he said, "I would be honored if you would consider speaking at our next Healthy Kitchens, Healthy Lives conference in February 2022, and sharing your journey. Would you be open to that?"

My hesitation, if even noticed by Dr. Eisenberg, lasted only a second but in that second the full weight and gravitas of the ask settled on me. I was being asked to take the same stage as those esteemed professors, chefs, dieticians, and researchers had just two years before. I was being asked to not just sit in the audience and take in but to stand from the stage and share. The honor felt surreal.

"Dr. Eisenberg—," I began.

"David," he corrected.

"David," I said. "Yes. One hundred times yes. And thank you."

"No, Stephen," he said. "Thank you."

I hung up the phone and stared for a few moments at the wall. Then I turned and looked directly into the greenhouse. The space was flourishing with towers of growth and trellised tomato vines. The sun was just beginning to come overhead and natural light flooded the space with warmth and invitation. As I turned, I took in the brand-new culinary operation. Here, in this space that used to be a storage room, was a fully commercial kitchen. And standing in the kitchen was a group of twelve students who, fully embracing the entrepreneurial mindset, were cooking and eating and laughing alongside our chef instructor.

This was one of those rare moments of calm where the peace and surrealism of the present invaded my reality and grounded me in the realization that we had arrived. But not only had we arrived, we now had so very far to go. And it was a beautiful thing because we were just getting started.

CHAPTER FIFTEEN

> *"CHCA's entrepreneurship program taught me more than business; it taught me to fail more, put first things first, be proactive, and embrace grit. More importantly, I learned that habits are life's foundation. Little actions yield intangible results. These lessons prepared me and continue to propel me as I take my next steps in life."*
>
> — Johnathan, '23

"It seemed like a good idea at the time" is my explanation for a lot of projects in life, and the decision to write a book, as the teaching kitchen was being built, as the greenhouse was coming together, as the curriculum for the program was being designed, and as I was teaching a number of classes, is one of those projects. If, however, we are endeavoring to teach students to actively seek out opportunities, we as educators must be willing to do the same in our lives. And I saw the opportunity.

I need to get better at seeking feedback. Feedback is, of course, essential to growth in any field, but the fact of the matter is, it hurts. It hurts to have someone tell you what you are doing wrong or not doing enough of. You would think that after eighteen years in a classroom with high school students you would be numb to constructive feedback, but it never stops stinging. Especially when it's true. Early in my career I passed out surveys at the end of the semester to gauge my performance as a teacher and I quickly decided that I would rather just not survey the students and assume they were all more than satisfied with the classroom experience.

Trust me, I know how this sounds. Here's the guy talking about growth mindset and thinking like an entrepreneur, and he's admitting to hating getting feedback. I wish I could say that I grew out of that and now I love getting feedback, but that's too far from the truth. What I can say is that I've come to accept the role of feedback and that the way it is sought can have a big impact on its value. This is why I started actively seeking feedback from the parents in our community around the entrepreneurship program. The students, it was clear, were our primary customers, but the parents were the ones paying. If we are to run our school like a business, we had to have satisfied customers. And it also turns out, parents are quick to point out what is not working well.

Thus began my mission to interview as many parents as possible regarding their experience at the school. Were they getting their money's worth? Could they justify the expense having seen the product firsthand? I tiered the feedback toward parents whose students were involved in the entrepreneurship program and asked questions like, "What was the most valuable learning for your student" and "Where could the program improve?" When I got to the improve question, by and large parents brought up the topic of financial literacy.

"How come we're not teaching personal finance?" they would ask. "I mean, my kid can talk all day about the periodic table of elements, but she can't figure out how to balance a checking account. Something seems off."

And off it was. After hearing this from countless parents, I began researching the school's approach to financial education. It seemed the subject had been outsourced to the economics class and was primarily taught with a focus on business finance. When it came to credit cards, personal investing, saving plans, and college loans, we were woefully underprepared as an educational institution. And it also seemed to me that the proper place for such a practical, important class was the entrepreneurship program.

We were teaching so many valuable skills in the entrepreneurship program and had structured our programming around the development of the entrepreneurial mindset. But we weren't teaching them to save like an entrepreneur. Or invest like an entrepreneur. Or create and maintain a budget like an entrepreneur. And it was clear that had to change. This kickstarted a research phase around financial literacy that led down a rabbit trail of books, resources, and curriculum that left me exhausted and unfulfilled. It's worth noting that personal finance has long been a passion of mine handed down to me by my frugal grandfather who instilled in me the wisdom of long-term investing and paying yourself first. I was sixteen years old when I first read *The Richest Man in Babylon* and I had grown up with the concept of compound interest firmly ingrained in my education.

And I wanted the same for my students. Perhaps it was my love of Patrick Lencioni books and the fable technique of Ken Blanchard, but I decided, then and there, that I was going to write a book that would teach the core principles of personal finance to young adults using a story, keeping their attention while driving home key truths. The books that teach me the most are the ones that keep my interest and I wanted to bring this to the world of personal finance for teens.

I'm also a believer in "don't break the chain." This technique, popularized through an anecdotal story about Jerry Seinfeld's joke-writing habits, involves taking a large yearly calendar and crossing off each day that you work on a particular project (or habit or goal). After a few days, you have a chain of x's, and you then work to not break the chain under any circumstances. Come hell or high water, that chain will not be broken. I decided to write five hundred words a day. Day after day. Every day. In the morning, at night, during lunch, or in between classes, I would write. A few sentences here, a paragraph there, and eventually the story started to come together.

I had been steadily working on this project for the last few months, and just as I was getting the news about the Teaching Kitchen Collaborative, *The Seed Tree: Wealth Building and Money Management Lessons for Teens* was published on Amazon. And like that, the financial literacy program took off at Cincinnati Hills Christian Academy. Everything that has grown in this program, from our horticulture classes to our culinary classes to our student-run businesses, has grown because of student interest and student engagement. Financial literacy has grown for the same reason—students are interested in this topic. Perhaps it's the nature of the educational system to, over the years, create jaded students who begin to question the legitimacy of an education steeped in archaic knowledge. Why spend weeks and weeks memorizing dates and figures and formulas if all this information was readily available on one's phone? Will we really use this concept that we are learning to help further our life?

Much of this comes down to value-add—does the concept we are studying directly add value to my life? If not, then most of our students will tune out. If yes, however, students will tune in and once you have students tuned in, you have grounds for exciting growth. Students began to take financial literacy and they started opening Roth IRAs and having conversations around the stock market and getting excited over compound interest. To those who may question whether a student could ever get excited around compound interest, I say come visit one of our classes—when compound interest is explained, and I mean *really* explained, almost visible light bulbs turn on and students get very excited.

Compound interest, the building block of any habit formation or goal-setting system worth its salt, is one of two primary concepts at work in all aspects of our entrepreneurship program. The second is opportunity cost, which is thoroughly explained later in this book, but suffice to say, its immediacy and practicality allure even the most cynical of students. Because of the success around financial literacy, the entrepreneurship program has now added an advanced investing course (which offers honors credit) to students who want and are ready for the next level. In the coming years, we will have a group of students who, after progressing through the financial literacy track, will run and operate an endowment fund making real trades in real time. And it's hard to imagine a more impactful, real-world experience than that.

CHAPTER SIXTEEN

"Within two years, Stephen Carter had conceived, designed, funded, built, and prototyped a teaching kitchen for use by K-12 students. One of his goals is to enable all students to 'eat, cook, move, and think more healthfully,' for their own health as well as the health of the planet they need to protect and sustain. Stephen is a visionary. And an entrepreneurial alchemist. And an inspiration to all who know and work with him!"

— David Eisenberg, MD
Director of Culinary Nutrition, Adjunct Associate Professor, Department of Nutrition
Harvard T.H. Chan School of Public Health

Returning to Napa for the 2022 Healthy Kitchens, Healthy Lives conference felt like a victory. Instead of coming solo, I was returning with not just our upper school principal but also one of our assistant principals and our full-time chef instructor. We were here not to gather research on starting a teaching kitchen but rather to share the experience of having created one and going on to become the first K–12 school in the Teaching Kitchen Collaborative. To say I entered the space with excitement would be a monumental understatement—I was on fire, more passionate than ever before.

David Eisenberg had scheduled me to speak the morning of the second day and when the time neared, I felt a series of nervous reactions. Not being one to get nervous before public speaking, I found this strange and a bit disconcerting. Old feelings of not belonging and imposter mentality began to creep in but just as I was starting to succumb, David took the stage.

"Next we will hear from a friend of mine who I met just two years ago right here on this stage."

He gestured to me.

"If you were here for the event," he continued, "you'll remember that Stephen stood up at the end, took the microphone, and announced his desire to start a teaching kitchen at his high school. Well, now he's here representing his school as the newest member of our collaborative."

David went on to tell more of the story and his warmth and generosity emanated so clearly that my nerves vanished as I sat listening to him. When he finished and I took the stage, I found myself filled with a passion and intensity that would become more and more familiar to me in the months and years that followed. What we were doing, day in and day out, through our elective classes and our internships and our experiences, was changing the lives of students. And those students were going to go out and change the world. In this way, real and tangible in every aspect, we were changing the world. With each wood-fired pizza and spring vegetable risotto, with each lesson on compound interest and discussion on habit formation, we were making a profound difference in the lives of our students.

And that feeling is intoxicating. It is inspiring. It is what we, as humans, strive for in our work. We long, internally, for something that has a clear purpose, something that brings with it a sense of fulfillment. In later years, as we would return to Healthy Kitchens, Healthy Lives, we would encounter others who, drawn to this sense of purpose, would ask, sometimes outright, for openings. They would ask for opportunities to be part of the story unfolding in Cincinnati and to have the chance to participate in the change being had.

This is primarily because everyone understood, and continues to understand, that this is about more than a culinary program or a financial class or a coffee bar or greenhouse. This is about a mindset and once that mindset is adopted, the world becomes more accessible and success more attainable. This is about instilling hope in the lives of the students and the teachers and the parents, and about spreading that hope through all we come into contact with. When I was first at Healthy Kitchens, Healthy Lives, I did not belong. Not really. But now, we were given a hero's welcome and a hearty dose of encouragement. In a flash, the last two years, mottled with COVID, plexiglass, lack of funding, unfinished spaces, stress, myriad frustrations, and more, all faded into one clear journey that brought us back to this spot.

After my talk I was approached by one of the program's speakers whose specialty is on teaching mindfulness.

"Stephen," he said, placing his hand on my shoulder. "I'm curious. You mentioned that you asked your administration for $1 million and in response they gave you $150."

I smiled and nodded in response.

"In retrospect," he continued, "would you say it was a blessing?"

"A blessing?" I asked.

"Yes, a blessing. Do you suppose it would have had the same success if you had been given the money up front and not had to work for it? If it had been easy and the students hadn't had to get scrappy to make it work?"

"I hadn't thought about it like that," I said, "but there's truth to it. Though it would have been a lot easier to have just been given the money."

"That's my point," he said. "It would have been easier. But it would have been far less powerful. And that's what this is—powerful. Thank you."

With that he shook my hand and disappeared into the crowd, leaving me to consider what would go on to be a defining attribute I would encourage other schools to adopt. Now when I'm asked how a school can start an entrepreneurship program, I always explain, after encouraging them to define their *why*, that it comes down to leadership. Identify who will lead the program and select the best person for the job. Then give them three things: freedom, autonomy, and resources. The only caveat is with resources—give them resources, but not too many. Give them funding, but only a little. Encourage scrappiness, build grittiness, and sit back and admire the results.

CHAPTER SEVENTEEN

"The entrepreneurship program is more than just a few classes to me - it helped guide me to what I really wanted to do, which is to focus on food waste and sustainability concepts. As a student who previously worked at the greenhouse, I got to work hands-on with crop production, learn sustainable actions which is not something you hear every day from high school. I valued my time being a participant in this program and I wouldn't have it any other way - in fact, I now major in Biology and Environmental Earth Science with a co-major in Sustainability."

— Faye, '21

From the beginning, it was clear that entrepreneurship and sustainability was shaping to be more than an academic program—it was grappling with larger ideas of how we teach and what we teach, of reaching learners who previously fell through the cracks of the educational system, of creating opportunities to truly learn new ways of thinking and approaching situations. In short, this was about mindset. Yet it was also apparent that we needed a way to systemize the learning to truly demonstrate what the students were taking away.

In the early days, it was easy to say that students working the coffee bar were learning valuable skills like effective communication (customer service, teamwork, etc.) and growth mindset (building a business from scratch and making it successful). But as the program grew and as new opportunities came around, like running a greenhouse business or operating a wood-fired pizza oven, the experiences began to vary. While we could definitively say that regardless of the business, the students involved were learning key skills, we could not necessarily say that the learnings were the same.

Keep in mind, however, that no one was breathing down our necks asking to see a curriculum map of the learning, but I lived in fear that one day we would get asked to show the specific learnings of the program and I'd struggle to show synchronicity between experiences. It was out of this that the first notion of the certificate track was born. If we were going to say that students who came through the program were developing the entrepreneurial mindset, and I was already saying this to parents and students alike, then it stood to reason we needed to clearly demonstrate how that mindset would be established. As we started adding electives apart from the primary internships, such as financial literacy, greenhouse systems, culinary foundations, and others, it would get harder and harder to say just exactly how students would come away with this advertised mindset.

Consider, for example, the parent who has heard that the entrepreneurship and sustainability program at CHCA teaches students growth mindset, grit, redefining failure, and opportunity seeking, so they enroll their student in one of the classes. At the end of the semester in, say, financial literacy, if that parent assumes that their student has fully grasped the core values inherent in the entrepreneurial mindset, we would have a problem. It would not be possible in any scenario to say that a mindset had been developed after a single semester course, no matter how engaging or practical the content. There needed to be a specific track outlining key courses and experiences that, once complete, would ensure that the students had had enough exposure to the entrepreneurial mindset that they could be said to have developed the mindset in themselves.

As with any primary academic change, there were many iterations before landing at our current model. In this model, the student comes in as a freshman or sophomore and takes our foundations course called Perspectives of Entrepreneurship. This course goes in depth on the entrepreneurial mindset, habit formation, goal setting, teamwork, and networking skills. Rather than teaching students how to start a business, it teaches them the foundational skills necessary to achieve success in any area including how to start a business. And after taking this class, students can then have their choice of "internship." This notion of the internship became the catchall for not only any student-run on-campus business (of which, at the time of this writing, there are six being run by students on campus) but also for internships at local businesses where students could earn course credit by working a set number of hours a semester. In expanding this to include local businesses, we were able to advertise that any student who requested an internship would be guaranteed to get one—a massive change since the days of limited spots at the coffee bar.

Each internship lasts a full school year, spanning two semesters, and certificate track students must complete two years of internships, for a total of four semesters. Additionally, they must take financial literacy (which, being online and self-paced, can be taken at any time and in any bell of the day) along with an additional elective of their choice. Their senior year, they complete a capstone project and then graduate with the "Certificate of Entrepreneurship," which includes a designation on their official transcript, special cords at graduation, and an end-of-the-year formal ceremony off-site. And in doing this, we created an opportunity for any student to take any of our classes but for the more serious entrepreneurially minded students to have a path toward developing the entrepreneurial mindset.

This, however, led to an additional problem. Once the certificate track was created, and we had a number of students progressing through the problem, completing internships and taking key electives, we still were not able to definitively say that they were learning the same things. They were *learning*, that was for sure, but to clearly define the experience was still lacking. If we had a student go through the certificate program using the coffee bar as an internship, that brought a different set of learnings than Eagle Farms, or Eagle Pizza, Co. In the early stages, with just a small handful of businesses, this differentiation of experience was easy to explain away as the experiences were so similar. As we grew, however, the learnings began to vary.

It was at this point, in trying to bridge these gaps, that I found myself at a lunch meeting with two representatives from a well-respected faith-based accelerator in Cincinnati whose primary mission is the fast-tracking of want-to-be entrepreneurs through a robust curriculum based in business training, biblical wisdom, and community connection. With this model, they worked with adults and helped them realize their dream of solving problems through entrepreneurship. As I explained what we were trying to do at CHCA with entrepreneurship and the entrepreneurial mindset, a sort of clarity came over the meeting.

"Why don't you let us help you," they said, listening intently to my story. "Don't reinvent the wheel."

I had just explained my desire to have a unified curriculum that was engaging enough to keep the attention of high school students while informative enough to teach key aspects of entrepreneurship.

"I would love your help," I said. "What does that look like?"

"We've developed the kind of curriculum you're discussing but we've developed it for adults. Why don't we work together to create this for high school students?"

The more we talked, the more the idea began to take place. I explained my passion for something engaging; rather than a typical, dry, boring online class, this would be modeled after what David Rogier had done with MasterClass. Each lesson would come with a high-quality video of five minutes or less that would be followed by a short article or reading assignment and quick assessment. The key would be the application. Instead of the typical class, where the learning remains wholly separate from the application (and the application is often years later, if at all), this would be immediate and meaningful: after the lesson, the students would be able to directly apply the learning in the business they were managing.

They listened and took notes and nodded occasionally. After I was done explaining my vision, they spoke.

"Do you have a set of key learnings or concepts you want covered?"

"I do," I said. "I have four primary attributes: growth mindset, grit, redefining failure, and opportunity seeking."

"Wow, you rattled those off fast."

"Those are our foundational attributes," I said. "It is what we are calling the entrepreneurial mindset. If we can weave those into the content, we'd be golden."

In the end, we ended up working together over the coming months to create two entire years of curriculum, made up of seventy-two total lessons, where students, once a week, would engage with a key concept before directly applying it to their business. And the beauty of the project was its scalability. Instead of having waiting lists and students who wanted to be involved in the program but couldn't, we now had unlimited spots for our students. If a student wanted an internship, they could work at one of the six businesses on our campus or they could set up an internship on their own or they could work with our partner businesses in the community. All they had to do was get in four hours a week and complete the online coursework.

The product ended up better than we ever anticipated. In another moment of full circle coming together, I was able to hire a former student of mine who runs a videography business out of Chicago who was in the original group operating the coffee cart prior to my involvement. Even just the rudimentary coffee cart operation had given him enough of a spark to pursue the entrepreneurial spirit in his own life and his business was thriving—but he was able to take the time to create masterpieces out of each video. The course flowed together with key learnings and student engagement soared—it was clear that the combination of entrepreneurial education with hands-on application was a winning formula. The year after our pilot program of implementation, we had a record number of applicants for internships, and we were finally able to claim, with confidence, that each student would receive an experience focused on a core set of learnings that was similar regardless of the internship. And out of this, the full breadth of the entrepreneurship certificate was born—the ability to demonstrate, with clear metrics and tangible experiences, that students emerged having developed the entrepreneurial mindset.

And we're not even close to being done.

In the weeks and months that followed the curriculum build, we began adding meaningful electives focused on creating student engagement and solving key problems with traditional education. Electives focused on our *why* as a program. Out of this deep dive, an opportunity surfaced—high school health. If we are teaching growth mindset, grit, redefining failure, and opportunity seeking, then we also have to set students up for lives of success and wellness so that their entrepreneurial mindset has a healthy body in which to operate. Health class, therefore, is central to entrepreneurship. And redefining that experience because of our primary goal. Thus began the quest to create "Elevated Wellness"—a class that takes place in three locations, rotating between our teaching kitchen, our greenhouse, and our school grounds. With three instructors, including our certified chef, our horticulture expert, and a newly hired wellness coach, students learn about healthy living not from a textbook but from the food they eat, how it is grown, and how it helps them move.

Before you ask for metrics and measurements on the success of the class, please know that the class, in its pilot version, is just now happening. But we are living out our ideology—in seeking new ways in which to engage our students and create excellence in our program, the true failure would have been not trying to solve the problem in the first place. I will say that in launching the class and attracting student interest, we ended up with a full roster for both semesters. This is in addition to offering a full slate of culinary courses, horticulture courses, financial literacy courses (topped off with an honors finance course called "Advanced Investing"), and marketing and sales. And all are full to the brim.

This is not a brag but rather a reflection of the belief that our students desperately want to be engaged in their learning—so much so that they will pursue it by whatever means necessary. And it is this that has been our driving force, our loadstone and compass. Are the decisions that we are making for the future of the program focused on student engagement around teaching the entrepreneurial mindset? If so, we forge ahead, undaunted by obstacles and roadblocks. We do not seek out smooth sailing and worry-free solutions. Instead, we push ourselves to think as big as possible. David Schwartz, in his famous book, *The Magic of Thinking Big*, tells the story of the three bricklayers. For our intents and purposes, let's say that the bricklayers are building a new school, one brick at a time. When someone walked up to the first bricklayer and asked, "What is it that you are doing?" the bricklayer responded, "I'm making $19 an hour." The second bricklayer was asked what he was doing, and he responded, "I'm building a school, one brick at a time." Finally, the third bricklayer was asked what he was doing, and he responded, "I'm helping build into the education of the future generation and offering them the chance to change the world." Years later, Simon

Sinek would capture this notion and call it "Start with Why"—and the concept remains true. If we, as educators, innovators, and instructors remember our *why*, our big idea, our third bricklayer mentality, then we are no longer just crafting academic programs. We are no longer building businesses and facilitating growth. We are, instead, changing the world, and we are doing it one student at a time.

It is this mentality, this sense of overarching purpose and calling, that keeps the program vibrant and alive. I have every reason to assume that five years from now, the program will have grown and changed and evolved to be larger and more influential than it is now, and the reason is that it is grounded in a meaning larger than itself. When we help students develop a mindset, we are helping them develop a way of life. And when we help them develop a way of life, we are helping them approach the world in a new way, fresh with ideas and solutions to counter the inevitable problems they will face. And in this way, we are paving the way for the successes of the future.

Other schools are getting on board. After fielding countless emails with questions around our programming and curriculum, I finally took the leap into consulting and began working with administrators on incorporating this mindset into their institutions. What school leader, after all, would not want to pursue student engagement as a measure of success? And the results speak for themselves. As I write these words, we are facing the largest number of students both in specific internships as well as in all elective courses than we have ever faced. The students are voting and their course request form acts as their ballot—with each entrepreneurship course selected, a vote of confidence is cast.

It is for the reason I love what I do—I believe that when you change a person's mindset for the better, you impact their entire life. And these students, in turn, go out and impact the world. When it comes to having a personal *why*, I can think of nothing more inspirational than getting up each and every day charged with the immensely important task of impacting lives through the development of a mindset. And that's what I mean when I say we're just getting started.

PART TWO
THE ATTRIBUTES OF THE ENTREPRENEURIAL MINDSET

Back in 1998, Spencer Johnson published his famous work, *Who Moved My Cheese?* In it, he tells the story of Hem and Haw, two mice who face the startling dilemma of a dearth of their cheese supply. While one mouse uses this problem as an opportunity to seek out new sources of cheese, the other succumbs to despair and presumably starves to death, though the ending is left open to interpretation. In education, perhaps more than in any other field, we collectively fight against change. Change is scary—it brings about the unknown and foists upon us changes and developments that are unforeseen and stretch us in uncomfortable ways.

Consider the teacher who has taught the same unit for twenty years with little to no change. While two decades of research have emerged and learning styles have shifted and attentiveness has waned, she still dutifully plugs away with something created before the dawn of the iPhone. Unfortunately, this often ends up being more common than not. And our students pay the price for it. As an increasing body of research sheds light on how our students now think and learn and what they value regarding their learning, we begin to erode the very fabric of their interest in lifelong learning and growth if we continue to offer these lessons. After all, how can we convince our students to continue to learn later in life if learning now is associated with boredom?

Our students do not want to sit in traditional classrooms, lined up in traditional desks, perched in traditional chairs. They do not want traditional lessons from traditional teachers with traditional units situated within traditional subjects. They want more. We're dealing with a generation who is facing real change—global warming is a reality with repercussions they will deal with for the duration of their lives. Traditional workplace environments have imploded, and the gig economy continues to pull away desk workers as more and more pursue side hustles. They want nothing to do with a traditional school. So why, then, do we continue to offer this product?

The same mice who stay back and slowly starve to death are the ones sitting in the corner trying to protect their "time-tested" methods while the very fabric of education changes. These are the educators afraid of change, afraid of the unknown. These are the educators who panicked when calculators became the norm, when Google began to answer complex questions, when cell phones began appearing in pockets. Don't even get them started on ChatGPT. These are the educators fighting against the future and we know that all who have fought against the future have lost—the past is where forward thinking goes to die.

I often work with schools that say, "We don't have a four-thousand-square-foot greenhouse or a teaching kitchen. How can we start?" The answer? With a few pieces of wood and some wheels. With $150 and an innovative idea. With a few sketches on a restaurant napkin. And unifying all of this is with a group of students. Students who want more than the traditional experience and who are willing to venture into the unknown armed only with enthusiasm for change. Let them try. Let them fail. Let them strive to solve a problem that will directly impact a life, and in so doing, impact their own lives. Let them take ownership. Let them build confidence. Let them investigate the void and say not only "I can" but also "I will." Let them develop leadership, teamwork, curiosity, problem-solving, and networking skills. Have them versed in growth mindset. Enable them to build their grit and resolve. Teach them to redefine failure. Have them chase down opportunity. Encourage them to act with generosity and empathy. Create ways for them to become more effective at communication.

In other words, teach them to think like an entrepreneur.

Education needs to be about more than just transfer of knowledge. Education in the future needs to be about wellness—about finding purpose and calling within a society that works diligently to strip away our wholeness. Imagine an education where wellness comes alongside knowledge comes alongside practical training and comes alongside opportunity. Imagine an education where students are not only encouraged to become whole but are given a clear path to do so. We don't have to sit in the corner, afraid of the ever-changing world and the shape of education within it. Instead, we can create the educational experience of the future—they say that the best way to predict the future is to invent it. So, let's take the leap.

INTRODUCTION

"The CHCA entrepreneurship program taught me what it takes to curate a business idea and bring it to fruition. I was able to develop leadership qualities and skills that have helped me immensely in advancing my own career. The program gave me real world experience at heading up a concept, bringing it to life, and sustaining it, and what grit and hard work can accomplish."

— Max Vonderhaar, '21

Look around. Every independent school in every city has an athletic program. They all have a fine arts program. They have traditional academic departments ranging from English and math to social studies and science. Some are better than others, no doubt about it. And it's certainly a worthwhile investment to build into these programs and improve them. But in the end, it's a red ocean. The redder the ocean becomes, the more sharks appear and, in turn, the redder it ends up being until we can see no other color. If everyone is fighting for the same level of excellence, then everyone is fighting for the same distinction and then, in the end, no one stands out.

Instead, let's look to the blue ocean. Look to the idea that differentiates the school and sets it apart from the competition. In a way, this is a purple cow. Before Seth Godin's famous marketing book *Purple Cow: Transform Your Business by Being Remarkable* hit the market, we were first treated to the concept of the purple cow in a short 1895 poem by Gelett Burgess:

I never saw a purple cow,

I never hope to see one;

But I can tell you, anyhow,

I'd rather see than be one.

Burgess makes a fair point—being a purple cow means standing out and having people take notice of you. But this can also be a good thing. Godin falls on the positive side of the purple cow and recommends that businesses need to both identify their purple cow and then go all in with promoting it. The purple cow is the differentiator—after all, who wouldn't stop at the side of the road to take a picture of something so extraordinary? Businesses that take the time to identify and then promote their purple cow are businesses that will be visible in a day and age when traditional methods of marketing have failed.

As schools, we are more in need of purple cows than ever before. With educational choice on the rise from home school to micro schools, parents and students have more opportunity than ever before to create a customized educational experience and, in the end, it will be the differentiators that determine the feasibility of a school's future. Additionally, students are seeking more meaning from their education. They are growing cynical toward a $100,000 and up college degree, and they are hearing horror stories about the changing job market. If education is to adapt, then it needs to shift from transfer of knowledge to development of mindset. And nowhere is this mindset more important than in the space of entrepreneurship.

When we think about the attributes that make entrepreneurs successful, it is these same qualities that bring about success in all areas of life. We chart it up to creativity, independence, teamwork, vision, leadership, risk-taking, and more, and we often talk about these attributes in the same reverential tone we use when talking about critical thinking. Yet all too often, in our attempt to do too much, we end up doing nothing.

It doesn't have to be this difficult. Over the ten-year growth and development of our entrepreneurship and sustainability program, we have synthesized the concept of the entrepreneurial mindset into four primary core attributes. Infusing these core attributes into all parts of our programming, from the internships to the individual elective courses to the events, has driven student engagement as well as enrollment metrics. The following section of this book is dedicated to exploring, in depth, these core attributes. And the order matters—each attribute builds on the previous one, enabling the student (or teacher or parent or administrator) to strengthen the foundation with each successive component. In the end, it is the individual who thinks like an entrepreneur who will experience more success and fulfillment in life.

ATTRIBUTE ONE: GROWTH MINDSET

Much has been said about growth mindset in the past few years and no one has explored it more thoroughly than Carol Dweck. Her 2006 book, *Mindset: The New Psychology of Success*, has not only shaped and redefined how we teach but also how we understand the nature of education altogether. She defines the concept in the following manner: "In a growth mindset, people believe that their most basic abilities can be developed through dedication and hard work—brains and talent are just the starting point. This view creates a love of learning and a resilience that is essential for great accomplishment." This love of learning and resilience is key to understanding the benefits of this way of thinking. Collectively, we are all born into a growth mindset. It is inherent in young children to strive for growth and to work as hard as possible to achieve this growth. Imagine the child, trying to crawl for the first time and, finding it difficult, giving up and never attempting again. Imagine that child proclaiming herself to be a failure and simply accepting the inability to grow. It's a preposterous concept. We push ourselves to crawl and then to walk and eventually to run. We embrace our inherent growth mindset as we learn to think and then to speak and then to write. At any point, it would have made sense to give up because of the difficulty in learning these skills, but yet we persevered because of an inherent drive and belief in our ability.

The fact that we innately have an early growth mindset full of possibilities makes it all the more frustrating that, almost universally, we slip into a fixed mindset. When operating in a fixed mindset, Dweck explains, "People believe their basic qualities, like their intelligence or talent, are simply fixed traits. They spend their time documenting their intelligence or talent instead of developing them. They also believe that talent alone creates success—without effort." Maybe it is junior high when we face difficulties in new academic matters and start to doubt our abilities. Perhaps it is in upper elementary school when we develop slower than other students and question our athletic prowess. Or even in lower elementary when we notice other students grasping the content more quickly than we do. Regardless, society eventually pushes us into a mindset that says "can't." This mindset adds the negative word "not" to every modal verb form we have including can, could, should, will, and so on. When these positive words are turned into their counterparts, we begin to say we can't, we couldn't, we shouldn't, and we won't.

Dweck's work explores the ways in which we, as educators, can encourage students to move from this fixed mindset *back into* a growth mindset that centers on the notion "I can." It takes the idea that for students to do this, they must adopt the phrase "not yet" in place of "can't" or "fail." A "not yet" attitude suggests progress and forward movement; it suggests the belief of ability in the future. And this positive suggestion leads to the optimistic nature of a growth mindset. The beauty of the growth mindset is that it never has an endpoint—the nature of the mindset suggests that we work to adopt the philosophy that we are embroiled in a lifelong pursuit of learning, realizing that we will never "arrive" but that the journey itself contains the rewards. As educators, we often talk about creating lifelong learners in our students, but then we go right around and encourage (often unintentionally) a fixed mindset.

Nothing could be more detrimental to the notion of the lifelong learner than a fixed mindset. We live in a time where research tells us that more and more students, upon graduating from college, will never read another book in their lives—where AirPods blast playlists instead of audiobooks and where binge-watching television shows and spending hours on YouTube is considered the norm. In this state of things, imagine the impact on the world created by a group of students passionate about learning and growing and improving. And imagine if this passion continued throughout their entire lives.

One of the mantras inherent in teaching the entrepreneurial mindset involves the *why*. We must believe, wholeheartedly, that we are changing lives for the better. Every day we are having clear, tangible impact on the future success of our students. Rather than having to wait ten or fifteen years to see these results, we see them almost immediately through the flipping of the mindset switch. This is not to say that the changes are immediate, but the process to bring about the change is. Then, with the proper adherence to habit formation, the process becomes embedded and second nature. It is through this process that we arrive at an even larger *why* to inspire our methods: We are changing lives through our program and the lives that we are changing will in turn go out and change the world. Imagine a calling where you are changing the world—now imagine a school filled with faculty who truly believe they are, each and every day, changing the world. The great truth here is that the belief that what you are doing will change the world is often the very thing that does in fact end up changing the world.

Even as adults, we could do with regular doses of the growth mindset. We could use a little more learning and growing and improving. One might even go so far as to say that we cannot instruct our students in the growth mindset until we model it ourselves daily. And Dweck is quick to point out that the notion is not an either/or but is instead a spectrum. Rather than wholly operating in a fixed mindset or solely living in a growth mindset, we are situated somewhere on the long spectrum between the two extremes. The role of the educator, then, is to provide the tools and external stimuli to help students begin to move ever closer to the growth mindset end of the spectrum. The movement will be small at first, perhaps even minuscule in nature, but it will pick up speed and momentum once going. The principle of the flywheel is at work here—an enormous mass requires an excessive amount of force to just barely inch it forward. The force must continue in an unstopping powerful wave just to get the wheel to slowly turn but, as it begins to turn, it will turn faster and faster with less and less force. Eventually, the wheel will be rolling along nicely with just an average amount of force applied.

It is at this point that onlookers will say, "Hey, how did you do that so easily?" Of course, it was not easy, but as most demonstrations of success often suggest, it appears easy to those not in the know. Moving toward the growth mindset is certainly not easy. Moving toward the growth mindset is a daily struggle, an uphill climb, a certifiably difficult attempt to change one's way of thinking and accept possibility over complacency. But the daily pursuit of the growth mindset grows, slowly and over time, into a habit and that habit grows into a mindset and that mindset grows into a belief system and that belief system brings about extraordinary results. Before long, others will look and say, "Why do they have it so easy? Why do they get everything they want?" And of course, to them, it does appear easy, but to us, who have been laboring away at the flywheel, it is a long, tedious work in progress.

The more we embed this style of thinking, this "I can" attitude, into our regular thought process, the more problems will become opportunities. This will change our outlook as well as our perception and will therefore effectively change our entire life. In the end, it is growth mindset, more than anything else, that lays the foundation for what it means to think like an entrepreneur.

GROWTH MINDSET STRATEGIES:

It is impossible to teach growth mindset without first demonstrating it. This seems straightforward and simplistic, but it is entirely true. The strategy, therefore, regarding its implementation into schools is clear—demonstrate it. Through and through, day after day, model a growth mindset. Be intentional about your own personal growth, hire people who are passionate about personal growth, create a culture that models personal growth—these are the strategies at play. And these strategies are rooted in an even deeper philosophy: to embrace growth mindset, we must begin by embracing our *why*.

Just about every school that I visit has a mission statement. Some even have a clear vision statement and a list of core values. Rarely, however, do I find a school where all of the people doing the school's most important work know and have internalized the mission, vision, and values. For a fun (and often telling) experiment, ask the following question to a random sample of ten people from your school: "Can you tell me why this school exists?" Follow it with, "Can you explain where we are going as a school?" Top it off with, "Can you tell me what we stand for?" These three questions cut to the root of the *why*. If we cannot answer why we exist, where we are going, or what we stand for, there is no foundation on which growth can take place.

When I am asked to consult with a school or to conduct professional development, I always start by asking the individual(s) to consider not just the *why* of their school but also their own *why*. I believe, wholeheartedly, that we must be firmly rooted in a clear understanding our own mission, vision, and values, and that those need to be in alignment with the mission, vision, and values of our place of work for that work to transcend a traditional job and truly become a calling. We want the same for our students—to find purpose and fulfillment in life, and therefore it is essential to help them make the move from work to calling.

When our mission, vision, and values are clearly established, they become the compass by which we can direct our growth. This is an important concept, because growth without direction is scattered and haphazard and can lead to disastrous results. Growth that is directed, however, becomes a powerful tool for engagement and success. And understanding our *why* is essential to creating this clarity around direction—it answers not only why we exist but also where we are going and what we stand for. This is the essence of demonstrating and then teaching mission, vision, and values. As educators, we must model this style of growth and encourage our students not to grow for the sake of growth but for the sake of purpose and clearly defined direction. Once our own *why* is clearly defined through our own mission, our vision, and our values, then we can begin to work with our students on doing the same. Before you ask whether it is possible for students to begin developing a personal mission and vision statement while in school, please know that in my experience, not only is it possible but the students are hungry for it.

Everyone craves purpose—and students in today's society are more subject than ever before to the prevailing notion of a meaningless existence. Not only should we actively fight against this, but we should also provide them the tools to do this effectively. These tools exist in the firm grounding of a personal mission, a personal vision, and personal core values. In our foundations of entrepreneurship class, our first unit is titled simply "MVV" for "Mission, Vision, Values." In this unit, we walk through the importance of having a *why* and breaking that why down into three questions: Why do you exist, where are you going, and what do you stand for? This turns into a multi-class project where the students apply critical thinking skills in order to drill down to the core values that drive them.

By demonstrating these tools, we are giving our students not only a firm grounding in their purpose, but also the ability to apply critical thinking to other areas. Take the "five whys" example of problem-solving. A young lady in the foundations class was asked to define her core values and she sheepishly asked if "jealousy" could be one. I asked her to break that down into a series of *whys*.

"Why do you say jealousy is a core value for you?" I asked.

"Well, because when I'm jealous of someone, it makes me work harder to beat them," she said.

"Why do you work harder to beat them?" I asked.

"Because I want to see if I can win."

"Why is winning so important to you?" I asked.

"Because it makes me better—if I wasn't trying to beat anyone, I wouldn't have the motivation to get better."

"Why do you need motivation to get better?" I asked.

"Because I like the competition."

And just like that, she had arrived at one of her core values: competitiveness. Simply by asking why until arriving at the root cause, she was able to drill down into what truly was meaningful to her. From this point on, she can direct her life through decisions and goal making to ensure that core value remains at the forefront.

Students as young as seventh grade and perhaps even younger can begin to identify their mission, their vision, and their values and often this is a discussion they take home and shapes an entire family's outlook. If a business has a mission statement, why not a family as well? Imagine the profound impact of a family dinner conversation based on identifying core values central to the family and connecting everyone's personal *why* to the overall *why* of the family unit. Such is the case with any group moving toward a clear direction—and it all starts with modeling this mindset for our students.

Once the *why* is firmly in place and we have identified our mission, vision, and values, it is time to consider the personal growth plan. As professionals engaged in the education of today's youth, our own personal growth plan is not a convenience or option but rather a fundamental part of our modeling of this important attribute. If we have no plan to grow, we can expect no growth. Our personal growth plan lays out the key areas of growth we are targeting and establishes the path we will take and the metrics we will use to measure success. This plan clearly demonstrates not only where we are now but where we are going and how long it will take to get there. It is our manifesto of growth and, therefore, essential.

People attending my workshops and seminars are occasionally confused when, right out of the gate, I start with mission, vision, values, and personal growth planning.

"What about the classroom strategies?" they ask.

"The classroom strategies," I say, "only work when the person relaying these strategies lives it out in his/her own life. And the key to that is having a plan."

A personal growth plan focuses on the key areas of life where growth is necessary to accomplish the vision (where are you going?). Therefore, a personal growth plan is only necessary if an individual knows where he/she is going and that is why starting with that step is necessary before the planning takes place. Every administrator, school leader, teacher, and coach would greatly benefit from having a personal growth plan firmly in place before suggesting that students under their supervision do the same.

There are countless tools to be found in order to create a personal growth plan, but the most important aspect to keep in mind is that the plan must be balanced. Dean Nicholas is often fond of describing an out-of-balance situation as a weightlifter who focuses only on one bicep, thus leaving the rest of the body underdeveloped. While the bicep will be impressive, it will serve only to emphasize the weakness of the rest of the body. Because of this, our plan for growth must use a holistic approach. Instead of focusing solely on our health, or just on our bank account, imagine the impact of targeting all key areas from spiritual to relational to intellectual to physical to financial to vocational. Imagine the impact of creating a vision for each of these areas and unifying that vision around our personal mission and then aligning it with our core values. Now we have a plan for growth that will touch all areas of our lives. A plan to create a life of meaning and impact that will do more for reaching today's youth than an entire semester's worth of carefully planned curriculum. The old adage of students watching *who you are* more fully than listening to *what you say* applies on every level here. We can talk about health all day long, but are we healthy? We can go on and on about the benefits of reading, but do we read? We can expound mightily on the need to create strong friendships, but do we actively engage our close friends with meaningful conversation?

Growth that is directed and in balance is growth that is strong and healthy and contagious. It is a beautiful experience to be around someone who is flourishing with personal growth, and this can encourage others to pursue similar experiences—especially in the classroom. This sort of growth leads to lifelong habits that compound over time to generate massive success. And the key here is the use of time.

The next step to fully embrace a growth mindset is to demonstrate an appreciation, outwardly and inwardly, for the power of time. Time is truly our most precious asset and a growth mindset outlook requires that this asset needs to be *invested* rather than merely *spent*. We, as educators, have an enormous responsibility to properly steward the time our students give us. Although they often have little to no say in the matter, they trust us with the minutes of their lives and all too often we fill those minutes with busy work or senseless projects. However, if we cherish our own time as a finite resource, more valuable than money, then we will start to protect our students' time. And they pick up on this. They know when we are spinning our wheels, wasting their time. Whether they manifest it or not, they will resent us for this in much in the same way that we will resent ourselves, whether we know it or not.

What this means for education, both in and outside the classroom, is clear: Don't be boring. Boredom is where learning goes to die and the death is horrible and grisly. We must abhor boring. To be boring is to waste not only your own time but that of those around you—and many of them are innocent victims who are unable to choose an alternative. The older I get, the more I realize the necessity of protecting my ever-diminishing resource of time, which is why I find myself leaving a lecture, sermon, or meeting that is not filling my life with value. One of the most frustrating violations of this is when I am forced to give some of this time to someone or something that does not warrant it—this happens when someone is given a portion of my time and does not prepare adequately or does not fill the time with as much value as possible. Because of this, I make sure that whenever I am given the enormous responsibility of someone's time, I work tirelessly to pack that time with value.

Wasting time is a sin—it is one thing to waste your own time but to waste the time of others is an egregious act. As educators, we must work to avoid this at all costs. This goes for all activities in which we engage students—we are being trusted with the precious moments of their lives and we must uphold this responsibility and keep it sacred. So, beyond all else, we cannot be boring. That bears repeating: Do not, under any circumstance, be boring. This is easier than it sounds when embracing entrepreneurial education. Its inherent nature, in its hands-on, innovative format, is to keep students engaged with meaningful and practical training that has a direct ROI on their lives. When in doubt, we should immerse our students in learning that provides them with tools to live a successful life—in doing this, we ensure that we are returning their time with value-add.

The valuable nature of time is directly related to the concept of compound interest, which is one of the first concepts we teach in the entrepreneurship program. Everything comes down to compound interest—either it is working for us or it is working against us. And the concept is not solely relegated to matters of money. Take any personal growth, habit formation, or goal-setting book written in the last twenty-five years and a crash course in the importance of understanding compound interest will be the thesis. The concept builds on the notion of tiny, small moments working together to create the larger mosaic. In other words, every action, no matter how small, is either making us better or making us worse.

With every bite we take, we are either becoming healthier or more at risk. With every step we take (or don't take), we are either becoming more physically fit or more sedentary. With every dollar we invest (or don't invest), we are either becoming more financially secure or more restricted by debt. The science remains the same—small, seemingly insignificant steps add up, over time, to great distances. The question we need to ask, then, is where do we want to end up? Do we want to end up with type 2 diabetes, an empty bank account, and a broken family? We don't just wake up one day to find this a reality—it is a series of steps on a particular path.

Andy Stanley chronicles this in *The Principle of the Path* and demonstrates how we are always moving toward a destination and unless we are intentional about the destination we want, we will end up somewhere we did not intend and most likely did not want. Intentionality goes a long way and when intentionality is paired with compound interest, the results exponentially grow. This is how millionaires are made in their forties and how quality of life extends into one's eighties. This is how we achieve "success" and continually increase our enjoyment of this miracle called life.

This is, then, why I am adamant about teaching compound interest to our students. I was fortunate enough to encounter the principle early enough in my own life that I was able to apply it as broadly as I could. When I was in college, my mother offered me a bribe—she promised $100 if I read *The Slight Edge* by Jeff Olson. One hundred dollars bought a lot of pizzas in 2002, so I took her up on the deal. Instead of reading the book, however, I devoured it—I savored it, I relished every lesson. I took careful note of how we are always moving, never standing still. I often speak of the fallacy of "status quo"—this idea of maintaining as is, keeping things as they are. There is no such thing as "status quo"—we are either improving or getting worse. There is no middle ground. Compound interest is either working for us or against us; we are either earning it or we are paying it. This is as true with our finances as it is with our health and intellect and friendships. The point of a growth mindset is to make the power of compound interest work *for* you as opposed to *against* you—this is the ideology we need to impress upon our students through the lives that we live.

The truth is we are always moving and the direction is either forward or backward, toward progress or toward decline. A few simple disciplines in any given area repeated over and over, day after day, and success is guaranteed. The formula works. Just as a small investment, over a long period, can grow into a great fortune, so too can small, important habits turn into massive goals. This is how books get written, how marathons get completed, how weight is lost, and how lives are changed—the formula of compound interest.

But compound interest relies on time. Once we move out of the lie of quick fixes and simple hacks to focus on the long term, we can see real accomplishment and philosophy change. And this involves understanding a second, powerful concept: opportunity cost. There's a reason why so much time is dedicated to these concepts with our first-year entrepreneurship students—they form the foundation of the ideology we want them to adopt as they develop their mindset while in the program. In other words, if we want them to embrace growth mindset, grit, redefining failure, and opportunity seeking as well as continue to develop other key attributes, then we start with compound interest. From compound interest, we move to opportunity cost. From there, we are ready to introduce the path to future growth.

When it comes to opportunity cost, the students will be inherently biased toward "already knowing it." The concept is introduced in economics and most students are familiar with it from a large-scale business perspective. Some will even be able to articulate the following definition: Opportunity cost is the lost potential gain on an investment because an alternative investment has been made. This definition is all well and good, but it does little to motivate or inspire our students. It relegates a life-changing concept to a multiple-choice answer on an outdated assessment model and ensures that they never apply it in a meaningful way to their life.

We must teach opportunity cost, but we must teach it differently. We must teach it with direct impact and with passion. If we, as the educators, truly believe in the power and importance of opportunity cost, it is guaranteed that our passion will inspire students to take note and get involved. And if anyone doesn't believe in the power and importance of opportunity cost (yet), then just keep reading. For the foundation of the entrepreneurial mindset, opportunity cost involves not just financial dealings but, more importantly, time. Consider the role of time in one's life. Time is the primary resource we can barter throughout our life and often this is in exchange for money. Although we call it work, it is essentially an exchange of time for money and the more valuable we make ourselves, the more money we can earn in exchange for our time. It is important for our students to understand that they do not get paid by the hour. Hourly pay is an illusion. We get paid based on the value we bring to the organization paying us. If the organization values us at $15 an hour, then we will get $15 an hour for our value. But if we work on making ourselves more valuable, then the time that we trade for money will inherently earn more for the same amount of time. If we have a finite resource at our disposal, why wouldn't we try to get as much as possible when we trade it? Such is the case with time. Rather than settle our entire life for an hourly rate for our time, why not make our time as valuable as possible to our employer so that we get more when we trade for it.

    This is where we find the value in pairing opportunity cost with the entrepreneurial mindset. Once we understand that our value directly corresponds to what we can get when we trade our time, we will work to make ourselves *more* valuable, which requires a growth mindset (value is not *fixed*). When it comes to the hiring process, growth mindset counts far more than degrees and certifications. And it all goes back to opportunity cost. But opportunity cost, like compound interest, has a flip side—when we trade our most valuable resource, time, for something less valuable, like meaningless entertainment, we cheapen our enjoyment of life. Consider the startingly average day for the American worker—get up (begrudgingly), get ready to go to work, grab an immensely unhealthy processed breakfast before heading out the door to swing by Starbucks on the way to work where, in a mind-numbing cubical, numbers are punched for eight hours (with plenty of breaks and water cooler complaining) before heading home, ordering a pizza, and binge-watching four hours of Netflix. Rinse and repeat, day after day, and you have a life. There's a reason that Thoreau's pronouncement that the "mass of men lead lives of quiet desperation" rings even more true in our society today—we have traded our most valuable resource, the minutes of our life, for a far less valuable reality. This is why most Americans hate their jobs and feel like they live lives robbed of meaning—*because they do!* Don't let your students fall into this trap; help them strive for more, starting now. And that begins with a firm understanding of opportunity cost.

Once we understand the basics of opportunity cost, we will be more likely to use our time wisely. The key to happiness and contentment in this life is to invest our time wisely so that we increase our opportunities for enjoyment. We can invest our time in our health by getting eight hours of sleep (yes, even as adults), by exercising four or five days a week, by eating healthy (everyone inherently knows what healthy eating means, we don't need to read entire libraries on the subject), and by spending time outside. We can invest our time in our value by working on our personal growth, by reading regularly, by listening to audiobooks (instead of inane music or angry radio commentators), by attending lectures, or by taking online classes. We can invest our time in our relationships by spending time with loved ones, planning dates with spouses, going on regular vacations, and connecting with friends. These are all investments of time—they are assets. As assets, they grow and increase our wealth—they make us happier and wealthier. If we do not invest our time but choose instead to waste it (social media, screen time, Netflix, reading trashy novels, video games), we have turned our time into a liability. Not only does it generate no benefit, but it will eventually cause us to have less time. Unhealthy habits turn into an unhealthy life, which turns into a shorter life and a life of far less quality. Like the

Principle of the Path, it is no surprise when we wake up one day to discover our body riddled with pain, with a lack of energy, and no inherent joy. That's a lifetime of wasting our time instead of investing it—a lifetime of ignoring the power of opportunity cost.

Like compound interest, opportunity cost works regardless of whether or not we are aware of it. It is always turning, like a ceaseless motor, and it is the wisest among us who decide to make it work for ourselves rather than against ourselves. Like the famous quote attributed to Einstein, "Compound interest [or opportunity cost] is the eighth wonder of the world. Those who understand it, earn it, and those who don't, pay it." Don't let your students develop into someone who pays it—with the right tools and education, they can earn it to an incredible degree and live lives that are full to bursting with meaning and joy and purpose. And it all starts with us setting the examples in our own lives. We can, and should, empower our students with a mindset that will adapt *with* the times so that they will survive and succeed *regardless* of the times. And this starts with our attitude in the classroom. If we operate with a "seize the day" and opportunistic attitude, then we pass that on vicariously to the students. If we demonstrate a growth mindset through applying compound interest to every aspect of our lives, striving to make every moment matter with a clear understanding of opportunity cost, our students will fall in step. It is up to us to make the change in our own lives that we want to see in theirs.

In the end, the surest strategy to encourage students to move from a fixed mindset to a growth mindset is to demonstrate firsthand the benefits of this transition. When students look at you, do they see someone weighed down by the frustrations of life, someone void of joy who is merely existing from day to day? Or do they see someone vibrantly alive, living each day to the full and soaking up each and every unforgiving minute? That strategy will impact more lives than a cleverly designed lesson plan ever could. It also enables us to move to the second attribute where we can help them become grittier each and every day.

ATTRIBUTE TWO: GRIT

When I was in fifth grade, I was obsessed with collecting pins. Lest you immediately label me in this venture, please understand that there was a group of us involved in this pursuit. We (my cohorts and I) would work endlessly through lawn mowing, babysitting, dog watching, and anything else to earn a few dollars. As an aside, there is a certain sadness in the fact that you rarely see fifth graders pushing lawn mowers up and down the street anymore—society has certainly changed. But nonetheless, the drive and motivation for these odd jobs was to purchase pins to add to the growing collection. When we would travel to special events for school, there were often pins available to purchase. I remember one specific time when, competing in an Odyssey of the Mind event, I found a booth that sold pins for $5 each. I pulled five crumpled dollar bills from their safekeeping place in my sock and endured the cashier's disgruntled look, complete with a "why are these damp?" question, just to add a single pin to my collection.

At its peak, I had close to twenty-five pins, each with a story and sacrifice. Each held special meaning and was part of the ongoing autobiography of my life. And my pride in my collection was apparent to all. It was especially apparent to my grandmother who, upon visiting one summer, was subjected to the eloquent demonstration of my pin collection. One by one, I went through my pins and explained where I was when I got it and how much it cost. I could even remember the specific yard I mowed or child I babysat to earn that pin. My grandmother, as most grandmothers are required to do, gushed at my enthusiasm. It should have been no surprise, then, that several weeks after her visit a package arrived addressed to me. Inside was a collection of no less than three hundred pins. Pins from around the world, pins of all shapes and sizes, pins of varying cost—my collection had just grown by over 1000 percent. Thanks to my grandmother I was, by all estimation on my part, the richest boy in the world. My pin collection blew my friends' collections out of the water, and I was the ultimate collector of all time. And I was thrilled.

Until I wasn't.

Within a few weeks, the box of pins, which also contained my own previous collection, was shoved into my closet with little to no intent of ever opening again. I found that I no longer cared about pins or collecting them or showing them off. For some reason, unbeknownst to me at the time, my love of pins had vanished. When my friends procured some new pin for their collection, I merely looked on and nodded. When my mother asked why I was no longer interested in purchasing pins when we were out and about, I merely said, "I'm saving my money." But the truth was, I no longer cared.

It wasn't until years later that the root cause for this sudden change of interest became clear. The twenty-five pins in my collection had been procured from hard work—their value was in direct relationship to the effort required to obtain them. The sweat from mowing yards, the time invested in babysitting, the work in walking neighbors' dogs—this was the work I had invested to get the physical reward. And as soon as I was given all the rewards without the effort, the pins lost their value. I realized that their value was not in their inherent worth but in what they meant to me and what I had sacrificed and endured to get them.

I came face-to-face with the correlation of effort and value, a concept often referred to as grit. Angela Duckworth, the leading expert on grit, defines the concept as the combination of "passion and perseverance toward long-term goals." Grit is when you keep going, after you want to give up. It's when you try something even when you know you might fail. It's when you fall down, but you push yourself back up, when you have every reason to stop but you keep going. Grit is the stuff that movies are made of, the very fabric of inspirational stories. No one talks about the person who gave up or took the easy route. They talk about the people who endured and went the distance.

There's a misconception in society that we want things to come easily or that it's nice when things are comfortable. This is simply not true. Hard work and determination are the building blocks of value, and accomplishments won without grit feel hollow and empty. Such is the case with the participation trophy movement—our attempt to have no child feel left out has robbed the entire event of value. If we are to turn the tide in our society toward the need to embrace grit and to lean into things that are hard, we need to start in our classrooms. This is the essence of the entrepreneurial mindset, and grit can only take root in the fertile ground of the growth mindset.

Where there is a growth mindset, there is room for the development of grit. And because growth mindset teaches us "I can" alongside "I will," the student will come to understand that it is not a matter of having grit or not having grit but rather of developing an attitude of grit. Like the spectrum of growth mindset, moving from fixed to growth, grit too has a range, and we can all work daily to move toward being grittier. And entrepreneurial education provides the perfect nontraditional classroom to explore our movement toward this end of the spectrum.

The return on investment is clear—no parent would ever say, when asked if they want their child to become grittier, "No thanks, we're good." Of course, we all want our children to be grittier in the same way that we want ourselves to be grittier. We all bemoan the current society producing soft children unaccustomed to hard work and effort. But here we have a chance to fix that—here we have a chance to reverse the trend. And when it comes to setting our students up for success, developing a growth mindset steeped in grittiness is more than an ample foundation.

And the truth is, our students desire it. Yes, there will be complaining and yes, there will be frustrations in the effort, but the value of the result will more than reward these difficulties. Our job is to help them learn to lean in and embrace it. And sometimes this is easiest when we get them out of their classrooms and into new environments. One such example of this comes from a trip a coworker and I embarked upon where we took twenty-four students to explore national parks in Utah and Arizona. When we arrived at Bryce Canyon Park and took in the soaring vistas complete with hoodoos and snow-covered trails, we were in awe of the beauty. The spell was only temporarily interrupted when a nearby park ranger greeted us. Kevin, my good friend and co-chaperone, and I approached the ranger to inquire about the most important hikes we should do while visiting the park.

"Well," he said, looking around, "most folks do the Navajo Loop Trail. It's about a mile and a half and is an easy to moderate hike. Not too difficult and lots to see."

Kevin went back to the group to explain our plans while I stayed and further questioned the ranger.

"Sir," I said, "suppose we aren't 'most folks.' Suppose we want a bit more. What's the bucket list hike here, the one that pushes you to the extreme?"

"Well," he said, pausing for effect, "that there's the Peek-A-Boo."

I expected him to laugh at his own joke—surely there was not a hike called "Peek-A-Boo" and if there was, surely it was not in the least difficult. He sensed my surprise and continued.

"Yep, I know what you're thinking. Sounds easy. Well, it's the hardest hike in the park and I only recommend it if you're up for something strenuous. But the views are the best around. Totally worth it."

Totally worth it, I thought. That's what we're looking for. I thanked him for his time and returned to the group. Kevin had just finished explaining the plans for the loop trail.

"Listen," I said, looking around. "Here's an idea. If you're up for a grand adventure that will take us to the most scenic views in the park, then I've got the hike for you."

The students looked on with interest mingled with skepticism—they were used to my shenanigans.

"What kind of hike?" one of them asked.

"The kind dreams are made of," I said, smiling. "The kind that ensures your legs will burn and your lungs will burst. The kind where we are not guaranteed to make it to the end, the kind where we will want to give up and quit but will keep going anyway."

In my mind, music was swelling as I shared these words, and I could picture the exact scene in the feature film they would make as I inspired these students to seize something larger and bigger than they could imagine. I continued to describe the difficulty and the pain and the hardships they would endure and then, after I was nearly out of breath from the descriptions, I said, "Who's with me?"

Silence.

"Uh," one of them said, "I think I'm sticking with Kevin on the loop trail."

"Me too," another said. "Doesn't sound like my kind of thing."

More and more rejected the idea and walked away until I was left with just six students standing firmly in front of me.

"We're in," Lucas said, looking around. "Let's do it."

And with that, we took off toward the Peek-A-Boo Loop Trail. The trail includes an elevation gain of over 1,500 feet and its strenuous five and a half miles include everything from peaks to canyon floors. And it was tough. We were out of breath struggling more than we would admit. The weather (we had come in January) was brutal and the uphill ascents seemed to never end.

And yet we pressed on. Step after step, rock after rock, narrow pass after narrow pass, we hiked the Peek-A-Boo Loop Trail and, when we finally reached the scenic peak featuring up-close hoodoos and arches, we paused to take in the beauty.

It's true that you could google an image of the view and see what we saw. What you couldn't do is feel what we felt. That view had value because it was *earned*—because it was born out of determination and effort. Because it came from our grit, which pushed our endurance to the limit and gave us a story to tell for the rest of our lives. Over the years since, these students have graduated and gone on with their lives but occasionally, our paths will cross. And when they do, we make eye contact, nod, and simply say, "Peek-A-Boo."

While a strenuous hike through a beautiful national park is certainly a wonderful place to work on developing grit, it is also not necessary. Grit can be developed in the humblest of places and in the most unexpected ways. It is also necessary to note, however, that one cannot *force* someone to develop grit. Of those twenty-four students, only six chose the hike. Now I would venture to guess that a decent number ended up wishing they had chosen it based on the stories the six told, but had I forced them to go, the experience would have been drastically different. Because it was their choice, their willingness became the driving force of the grit development.

The lesson is clear—in seeking to help our students develop grit, we need them to be willing to take the first step.

GRIT STRATEGIES:

Grit can be taught. This is the foundational concept we need to accept as educators—no matter where a student (or ourselves) may be on the spectrum of grit, we can all work (applied effort) to become *grittier*. But this sort of thinking exists only in a landscape where growth mindset is firmly in place—a fertile ground to begin applying Duckworth's formula: passion and perseverance toward long-term goals.

But teaching grit is certainly not easy. No one is naturally inclined to seek out difficulty. As a culture, we often seek comfort and ease over adversity. Entire books have been written on the epidemic of living a life free of stressors—of getting out of an air-conditioned car and into an air-conditioned school before returning to an air-conditioned home. The fact is, we need to shift our students from a culture of comfort into a culture that embraces hard things. Consider weightlifting—in the weight room, the athlete pushes his body to an extreme, literally tearing muscle fibers in the process. Through a series of reps spread over several sets, the muscles are worn down and beaten mercilessly. And then, and only then, are they allowed to rest. It is during this rest phase that growth happens—the muscles, as they begin to heal, enlarge, and define themselves more fully, thus further encouraging the weightlifter who then is driven to work harder, causing the muscles to develop even more.

On and on it goes until peak performance is reached. A key point here, however, is that the muscles are either always improving or always declining—as in growth mindset, there is no status quo. We are either getting stronger or getting weaker. Such is the case with grit. We are either encountering adversity and working through it, becoming grittier, or we are shirking difficulty in favor of comfort and becoming less gritty. Through this thinking, we can clearly see the correlation between embracing adversity and the ongoing process of continuous improvement in the development of grit. In this section, we'll consider an approach to entrepreneurship education where grit is developed as a by-product as students are encouraged to embrace hard things.

When I get asked whether or not grit can be taught, I always begin by explaining that my approach is not the teaching of grit but rather the teaching of goal setting. In the teaching of goal setting, and in laying a foundation for students to develop long-term goals, to clarify a path to accomplish those goals, and to encourage them to set new goals once accomplished, they inherently become grittier each and every day. A fantastic model for how to do this can be found in the book *The Four Disciplines of Execution*. This work provides a coherent framework that meshes perfectly with these grit-producing projects; the book's philosophy hinges on a few key attributes: first, a "Wildly Important Goal," or "WIG," that the team rallies around. Second, there is a clear "scoreboard" to track movement toward this WIG. Third, there are "lag measures," which are used to determine whether movement is being made, and finally there are "lead measures," which are the levers that create the movement. Out of this framework, the two most important concepts that will revolutionize the programming are the WIG and the lead measure.

The establishment of the WIG should be a team effort. We need to encourage our students to dream and to dream big, to understand that there is nothing wrong with a goal that is too large or requires too much effort. There should be a lengthy discussion, or a series of discussions, and there should be some back-and-forth arguing for different points of view. In the end, the team needs to agree on one primary goal that is both "wild" and "important." Encourage them to think of something that would give them a story to tell for years to come—something that would give them an amazing sense of pride and accomplishment. Once the WIG is established, it should be written down in a big way and posted somewhere intensely visible. This should be front and center for them daily and they should constantly be faced with their own primary focus. This WIG will also function as a lodestone—it will be their rock and defining point of energy when they are faced with the "whirlwind" of distractions that will come their way. As they launch their project, they will be torn in multiple directions and chase down a variety of ideas, but they must stay grounded in their WIG, asking themselves if this particular project moves them closer to it. If not, even if it is a good project, it must be discarded.

This can be hard—after all, many a good idea will come their way once they start dreaming big. People will approach with suggestions and opportunities, and they will be tempted to explore many of them. When this happens, it is wise to lean on the titans who have come before and paved the way for extreme success. One such titan, Warren Buffett, explains it like this: "The difference between successful people and really successful people is that really successful people say no to almost everything."

Another famous innovator, Steve Jobs, puts it this way: "I'm actually as proud of the things we haven't done as the things I have done. Innovation is saying no to one thousand things." This is the mindset we must pass on to our students, and we can do that through an unyielding focus on our WIG. And this focused drive is, in essence, a laboratory of grit. By saying no and staying focused, we become stronger, and our effort is more concentrated and we, essentially, become grittier. But for this to work, we, as the teachers and administrators, must demonstrate it in our own lives. How can we encourage our students to focus solely on one goal when we are drawn in multiple directions and can't stay focused? How can we demonstrate the development of grit if we give up on our own dreams and accept mediocrity in our lives? Keep in mind that our students are watching us closer than we think, and our actions truly will impact them more fully than any lecture or collection of quotes.

Our program has grown on the premise of WIGs—and the necessary lead measures to help them come to pass. The concept of the lead measure is perhaps the most valuable, and often overlooked, component of goal accomplishment. It is easy to focus on the lag measures—those assessments we get after the fact that tell us how we *did*. It's often harder to focus on the things we *do* that create the positive lag measures and move us toward our WIG. Because of this, a dedication to the lead measures is essential. In the development of our program, I established the WIG of becoming the first K–12 school in the world to join the world-renowned Teaching Kitchen Collaborative. The goal was especially lofty because at that point, we didn't even have a teaching kitchen. To accomplish the WIG, we had to first understand what qualified as a teaching kitchen, then figure out how to build it, then figure out how to pay for it, and then go out and do it. But the WIG didn't stop there—to join the collaborative, we had to have programming and students, and to do that we had to create an entire academic curriculum and bring on a new hire in the form of an executive chef. Even then, we had to entice students to take the course as an elective and then get enough students to justify the program's very existence. In other words, the task was daunting.

But this is where lead measures come into play. If the biggest factor in getting the kitchen built was funding, then I needed to make sure that I, as program director, was meeting with as many potential donors as possible. This becomes a lead measure—am I, every week, having lunch with a donor? If so, then I can check that box. If I fall behind because I get caught up in the whirlwind of email and meetings, then I don't meet my lead measure. This is where a system of accountability comes into play—and what better accountability than the students who are working alongside you. Create a recurring schedule of team meetings where you gather to report on your lead measures and hold each other accountable—if I wasn't meeting with donors, then I had to face the look of disappointment on my students' faces, and trust me, that was motivation enough.

Sometimes lead measures work in reverse—in other words, to make time to meet with donors, I had to start saying "no" to other things, like unrelated Zoom calls, non-WIG related meetings, and various other duties. Some of these things can be delegated (other duties) and others just need to be cut (lots of pointless meetings). When you have an all-important WIG, you must prioritize around it so that the lead measures become most important. And although all of this may seem wholly unrelated to strategies for grit development, it is truly what the entire exercise is about. If grit is passion and perseverance toward long-term goals, then what better way to develop it than around long-term goals that require perseverance. The passion will fade, but that's where the perseverance kicks in—and that's where grit is developed.

One helpful tool I've implemented in my own life is the weekly checklist. Every Sunday night, I sit down and look over my upcoming weekly calendar and my email inbox. Then I review my goals and make key decisions about how to use my time. Everything I put on my checklist *will* get done—it is a matter of priority. This means that any pressing obligation that comes in after my checklist is created becomes a secondary priority. If my WIG is getting a teaching kitchen built, then I'll prioritize meeting with the contractor, visiting another local teaching kitchen, and having lunch with a donor over *everything* else that comes up, no matter how urgent. In fact, on my checklist, I have written my WIG at the time—this is a key reminder that everything that goes on there must be a lead measure to move toward that goal and that anything else is a distraction. Accomplishing long-term goals is a matter of organization and prioritization, and when we teach these skills to our students, we are helping them develop grit as this prioritization enables us to stay on track with long-term focus to accomplish really large goals, one lead measure at a time.

Lag measures can also be helpful in identifying potential WIGs in entrepreneurship programming. One such example came not too long ago with our coffee bar. Historically, sales always picked up significantly toward the end of the first semester—this was due largely to our Christmas menu, which featured several student-designed drinks including our famous "Christmas hot chocolate" and an array of peppermint-flavored beverages. The Christmas menu was always a hit and led to at least a 50 percent increase in sales over the previous month.

Except for the first semester of 2022. The first semester of 2022, sales did not increase but rather decreased by about 20 percent. The numbers dropped consistently week after week and did not recover. These sales numbers are a classic example of a lag measure—they represent the sales from the past day or past week and give the team an indication of the health of the business. But they are not a lead measure—they are not something one can do to influence the overall WIG. It was clear something, however, had to be done.

It was here that we assembled the "dream team" of the coffee bar. Each student-run enterprise at any school needs a dream team—a group of about six or eight students who are fully bought in and energized around the success of the venture. When assembling the dream team, one is looking for students who are engaged and motivated, who are willing to put in the effort and care deeply about the business. We assembled the team and then I presented the data from the lag measures (sales numbers compared with previous years) and asked for their thoughts. We met several times and debated various causes and reasons and then rallied around several key suggestions. I gave them what is required for the entrepreneurial mindset to thrive—freedom, autonomy, and resources (but not too much of any).

"Present me with your plan," I said after our third brainstorming session. "If it is reasonable in cost and big in vision, I'm all in."

They came back a week later with five key points to address. They had identified two primary factors contributing to the dip in sales: lack of interest in the bar from students and inconsistency in drink preparation from the baristas. First, they wanted to remodel the bar all the way down to stripping the wood top and re-staining it. Second, they wanted to close the bar for the first two weeks of the second semester to do a deep dive into retraining. Third, they wanted to visit The Container Store and purchase all sorts of organizational items. Fourth, they wanted to enforce a stricter sense of excellence from all baristas. Fifth, they wanted to do a big announcement around the "new" coffee bar.

"Yes," I said. "A resounding yes to all. Now go do it."

They jumped into the process with passion and exuberance. And they illustrated the need, once again, for freedom, autonomy, and resources. Take The Container Store as an example—they asked if it was OK to purchase a few key items, and I gave them the program credit card and told them to get whatever they felt was necessary. They had a blast—imagine being sent on a spending spree where the control over what to purchase is totally in your hands. This is where a sense of ownership is fostered. And they didn't go overboard—when they sheepishly returned and began to apologize for spending close to $300, I laughed and explained that they could have spent more.

In the end, when they reopened the bar to the joy of the students (and relief to the under-caffeinated teachers), they displayed a true sense of pride and accomplishment. In other words, they demonstrated passion and perseverance for a long-term goal—that goal being an improvement in coffee bar sales, born out of lead measures (their five-point plan) and tested by lag measures (daily sales reports). Grit, in the end, is not something that can be taught outright—but it is something that can be developed as a by-product of our method of teaching. And the best way to develop it is by fully engaging in a project in which you have complete and total buy-in, in which you are given freedom, autonomy, and resources, and in which you are allowed to take a sense of ownership. This is the playing field of persistence, and discipline, and accomplishment, and this is where our students exponentially increase their grittiness.

It's also worth pointing out that once the goal is met, they need to immediately celebrate the success—throw a wild party, have fun, spend some money on their accomplishment—and then go right into setting a new goal. They need to see the long-term piece of grit development as an ongoing, forever-increasing path. Not that this is discouraging—just the opposite in fact. This is highly encouraging—they will see goal after goal after goal set and then accomplished and then set again. This is the process they will then instill into their lives as they go out and seek adversity with a smile knowing that this is the stuff the joy of life is built upon, and they have the necessary grit to thrive.

Perhaps the greatest example of this method of teaching grit as a by-product of goal setting comes from one of our most recent ventures. At the start of the 2022–2023 school year, we assembled a diverse team of six students including two sophomores, two juniors, and two seniors. In that team, two students had already completed two years of internship in the program, one had completed one year, and three were fresh out of the entrepreneurship foundations class. We worked with the counseling office to arrange for all six students to be in the same bell and then made sure I had the scheduling capacity to be available during that time period as I would be directly acting as their mentor. On the first day of the school year, I gave them the following charge:

"Listen carefully—I have chosen you specifically for this group because of the value you inherently bring. The reason you are special is because, over the course of this year, you are going to do something no other group of students has ever done. You are going to design a unique business, of your choosing, and you are going to personally oversee it from concept to implementation."

I paused for effect.

"In other words," I continued, "you are all now officially entrepreneurs. You are visionaries. You are ready to rock 'n' roll. Now get started."

What I didn't tell, up front, was that they were responsible not only for coming up with an idea and starting a business but also funding that business start. Rather than just supply them with $10,000 to jump off, I encouraged them to explore options and then gave them an opportunity to raise the necessary money. In order to do this, I charged them with running Eagle Pizza, Co., our wood-fired pizza business.

The business, whose origin I detailed earlier, was still quite popular at the school and had earned a reputation for amazing pizzas, so overseeing the business required only the time and effort of making and selling the pizzas. In addition to working on creating new concepts and eventually starting a whole new business, these students had to operate the wood-fired pizza business to generate the revenue they would later need. And although this wasn't exactly what they had signed up for, they dove in with enthusiasm. Given that this was early in the year, with a full schedule of football games ahead of them, the students were able to come together and kick off the year with stellar sales, which then gave them the encouragement they needed to begin the ideation stage.

We started by identifying our WIG, which took place over the course of a single class period. I guided the students in a dream big exercise where we considered what our massively big, overarching goal would be. They were enthusiastic about this because they had seen, firsthand, the recent impact of this on our Eagle Farms program where, after a dream big session, we had landed on the ambitious goal of selling our produce to a local restaurant. What we discovered, in a matter of weeks, was that the goal had not been large enough—after arriving at the charge to sell to a restaurant, two young ladies on the business team reached out to a hugely successful restaurant located across the street from the greenhouse. These two students talked the produce manager into coming to the space for a tour and within the month, they had struck a deal to sell a large supply of bibb and romaine lettuce to the restaurant. They capped the deal off by negotiating the placement of an Eagle Farms branded sticker on every restaurant menu. The dividends from this in terms of program visibility continue to this day.

Armed with this tangible experience, the goal brainstorming session with the wood-fired pizza group was designed to go much larger than anyone thought possible.

"How about a food truck?" one student said. "We could take the pizza concept and go mobile with it, maybe even set up at birthday parties and graduation parties."

"Or maybe even a permanent pizza place," another suggested. "Then we could have DoorDash and delivery services."

"Let's scrap the whole pizza idea and dream even bigger," another said.

"Pasta," one student suggested. "We make homemade pasta and sell it."

"Too small," another said. "We need a larger goal, something really big."

"Maybe an amount of money?" someone said. "Like a goal to make $500,000 or something?"

"Possibly," another said, "but it doesn't sound that cool."

The dialogue went back and forth, and I occasionally contributed, suggesting that they step outside their ideas to think even bigger.

"How about a news story," someone finally said. "Like a big story from channel 12."

"Channel 12 already did a story on the program," someone said. "Last year—a special on the teaching kitchen."

It was true that several local news programs had visited over the past few years featuring the coffee bar, and then the greenhouse, and finally the teaching kitchen. The collaboration with Harvard University and the Culinary Institute of America had sparked considerable interest.

"What if it wasn't local news," another student said. "What if it was something with a larger audience, like national news."

"Yeah, like *Oprah*!"

"Or *Good Morning America*!"

The students began to rally with excitement, and it was clear we had landed on something big. Something profound. Something to work toward. By the end of the class period we had written, in large block letters, the following Wildly Important Goal:

"Get featured on *Good Morning America*."

"Now," I said, once the dust had settled, "let's figure out how to get there."

The students agreed that, while certainly cool, the wood-fired pizza business was less likely to attract the attention of a national news outlet than something else, something more original that had not been attempted by a group of high school students. As the brainstorming continued, one primary idea began to rise to the surface.

"Fine dining," one of the students said in a moment of silence. "A sort of supper club, a special opportunity where we turn this space"—he gestured around the teaching kitchen—"into a pop-up, four-star restaurant."

Andrew, the student who had spoken, knew his calling was to be a chef. And not just any chef but, like Max before him, a future Michelin star chef. It was no secret that Andrew had come to CHCA solely because of the entrepreneurship program and the culinary opportunities it provided. Over the course of the next ten minutes, Andrew explained, in great and specific detail, the far reaches of his dream and I watched as all five other students fell under his spell and agreed to put all their efforts into this plan.

The story of the next six months warrants a book in and of itself, but suffice to say that after extensive market research, recipe testing, budget planning, and menu marketing, the students launched the CHCA Fine Dining Club and sold out their first event to twenty people at the impressive cost of $200 a seat. As the date of the grand opening approached, I began to witness a spectacular transformation in the students.

This group, who had done a fine job of operating Eagle Pizza, Co. over the first semester of the year, came together to form a finely tuned dining operation whose careful attention to detail and adherence to specialty plating and exquisite preparation paved the way for a phenomenal grand opening. The guests, once they entered the transformed space, knew immediately they were in for a special opportunity as they were hand served canapes in the greenhouse before being seated at a family-style table with an amuse-bouche involving caviar. As they progressed through six courses, each impeccably introduced by the students, they began to fall into the magic of the evening, watching in amazement as the six worked together in a symphony-like arrangement to pull off a perfect event. As the guests left, at the end, the smiles were abundant and even more impressive was the look of accomplishment plastered on the faces of the students. They saw, in a firsthand manner, the power of the growth mindset, as they applied their efforts to a goal and then saw that goal come to fruition.

As of the writing of this book, the students have yet to be featured on *Good Morning America*, but we are not discouraged for we know that in working toward the goal, we are continuing to innovate and create moments of excellence where we can fully bask in the rewards of the growth mindset. The formula works—take an engaged mentor, add in a group of students with an entrepreneurial mindset (which can be established in a foundations class), establish a Wildly Important Goal, determine the lead measures necessary, and get to work. Student engagement becomes the driver and while the journey itself will be highly rewarding, the learning inherent in the experience (from goal setting to teamwork to ideation to creation) will foster lifelong growth.

The key to all of this is to first start and then continue the process. And this only happens when we embrace hard things—doing hard things simply because they are hard. A lovely verse in the New Testament book of James states, "Count it all joy … when you meet trials of various kinds, for you know that the testing of your faith produces steadfastness." I'm especially drawn to this verse because of how contrary it runs to our ingrained thinking. Instead of encouraging us to endure trials and make the best of things (lemonade out of lemons, anyone?), this verse specifically tells us to "count it all *joy*." Wow—imagine that mindset. Here's a trial, here's a difficulty, here's a dose of adversity, and we are admonished to celebrate and rejoice at the opportunity to deal with it. Sheesh—just picture what our outlook would be like if we celebrated at every opportunity to overcome a tough situation. That, to me, is pure grit. That, to me, is the stuff inspiration is made of.

I'm also drawn to the word *steadfastness*—in this context, it means "the quality of being resolutely or dutifully firm, unwavering." It is essentially a fancy word for grit. For determination. For resolve. It reminds me of the scene from the film *300* where the Spartans face down the arrows of the Persian army knowing that if, in fact, their arrows "blot out the sun," then they will "fight in the shade." Picture meet the teacher night in your building and, as you are welcoming the parents to a brand-new school year, you face the crowd and announce, "Your student, while enrolled in our classes, will learn, in addition to the usual subjects and lessons, the principle of steadfastness. She will understand what it means to endure difficulty and will embrace the entrepreneurial mindset while ultimately working toward the value of effort. She will, in short, develop grit." Clearly, standing ovations will be in order.

When it comes to developing classroom strategies to encourage students to become grittier, we must begin by restructuring the intent itself. We must see grit as a by-product, as something that is developed, almost accidentally, by pursuing long-term goals the students are passionate about and that require ongoing perseverance to accomplish. As teachers, we move from overseer and director to mentor and guide and the students, as they work toward the Wildly Important Goal, and as they establish lead measures to accomplish the goal, will discover that in the process, they have become far grittier than ever imagined.

ATTRIBUTE THREE: REDEFINING FAILURE

It's trendy in educational circles to talk about "embracing the learning experience of failure" or "teaching students to not fear failure," but at the end of the day, it's the same old story: We're afraid. When we do a cost-benefit analysis, we tend to overload the cost side and assume it is not worth the risk. When we consider our shareholders, our customers, and our employees, we decide to play it safe and minimize damage. Playing it safe can certainly be appealing—especially in the independent school arena. When the school board looks at enrollment numbers and makes a direct comparison to customer satisfaction in the classroom, it can be enticing to continue to rely on tested methods of the past. It can be enticing to avoid failure at all costs. It can be enticing to stay comfortable.

But comfort is the enemy of progress. Consider one of the greatest "failures" in Greek mythology: the flight of Icarus. Joined by his father, Daedalus, Icarus donned feathered wings to escape the labyrinth. He was instructed to avoid flying too close to the sun lest the heat melt the wax adhering the feathers to his body. This advice was well and good, but Icarus, once aloft and under the intoxicating influence of flight, tests the boundaries and, inevitably, flies too close to the sun. The wax melts and he falls to the sea to meet his drowning fate.

Alas, we say, Icarus fell. Icarus disobeyed. Icarus failed.

Except we are forgetting one key fact—Icarus flew. Icarus soared above the clouds and touched the very fabric of the heavens. Who among us can say the same about ourselves? Who among us would have stayed in the labyrinth for fear of potential failure?

The speaker in Jack Gilbert's poem "Failing and Flying" draws attention to this fact and then compares Icarus falling to a marriage failing. People focus on the pain of the divorce instead of the beauty of the love that preceded it. People focus on the fall and forget all about the flight. People say Icarus failed and ignore his reaching for glory. Of this, the speaker states, "But anything worth doing is worth doing badly ... How can they say the marriage failed?" Indeed, how can anything be labeled a failure if it merely came at the end of an attempt at greatness? Gilbert's poem concludes with the following lines: "I believe Icarus was not failing as he fell, but just coming to the end of his triumph."

This sort of thinking requires an inherent redefining of the word "failure" itself. Consider the following: As children, we are instructed through both literal words and powerful actions that failure is bad. We are taught that to fail is not to succeed and that one does not want to fail; therefore, one wants to ensure success. The best way to ensure success is not to try in the first place. This thinking is deeply ingrained in us and, over time, becomes the emotional response that unconsciously accompanies the very mention of the word "failure." No matter how many times, later in life, we may be told that failure is, in fact, good and should be celebrated, we are unable to get past the emotional underpinning of "failure is bad." If we dig down, we discover a logical syllogism:

Failure is not succeeding, and failure is bad; therefore, not succeeding is bad.

This is the state of things. Try as we might, we cannot overcome decades of indoctrination to convince ourselves that failure is actually good. Trust me, I've tried. No one wants to jump up and down in celebration of failure. It is, as it has always been asserted, bad. The easier approach, and the approach more likely to stick, is to redefine the word "failure" itself. Keep the negative emotional response with the word "failure" and change the definition to "not trying in the first place":

Failure is not trying in the first place, and failure is bad; therefore, not trying in the first place is bad.

In the end, we're not going to convince an entire population that failure is a good thing, and although it may be overly optimistic to think that we can convince them to redefine the word, redefining (an act that lives in the intellect) is easier than overhauling an emotional response (which lives in the heart and in the gut). It is especially possible if we begin the approach when our students are young.

Sara Blakely—American businesswoman, philanthropist, and founder of Spanx—shares in her MasterClass on entrepreneurship how her father, around the dinner table, would regularly ask the family what they failed in that week. Did they try out for something that didn't work? Did they make an attempt that turned into a disaster? If they had nothing to share, he would be visibly upset. What Blakely realized, years and years later, was that he had been reconditioning them to think of failure differently. He had been subtly altering the intrinsic definition of the word to mean "not trying in the first place." He had been helping them realize that what she should avoid is the regret that comes from missed opportunities.

Armed with this definition, we now avoid failure by *trying* or *attempting*. We must avoid, at all costs, not trying in the first place. Not trying in the first place is the breeding ground of regret—a sentiment shared by journalist Sydney J. Harris who stated, "Regret for the things we did can be tempered by time; it is regret for the things we did not do that is inconsolable." Consider your own history—are the heartstrings of regret pulled more at the things you tried without success or at the things you never tried in the first place? By altering the very definition of failure, we are offering our teachers and our students the opportunity to live a life free from inconsolable regret.

We, as educators, have considerable power at our disposal. Ours is truly a noble calling—we are given the opportunity to influence the mindset of future generations. It is up to us to give them the tools they will need to succeed in an ever-changing world—as disruption strikes and industries collapse, our students will be at a severe disadvantage if they define failure traditionally *and* fear the concept itself. By altering one of these aspects, we give them not only hope but an ability to thrive in the uncertainty, an unshakeable willingness to make attempt after attempt after attempt on the path to success. This also means, however, that we become willing to release our hold on results and outcomes as the sole measures for success. Our focus must shift to the process—try, not succeed, try, not succeed, try, succeed—rather than a desired outcome based on a time restraint. This is, in short, a mindset shift within our entire educational culture—we get the results that we measure, and if we shift what we measure, the results will follow.

    We will make mistakes. We will try things that will not work out. We will start programs that will wither and die. This, however, is not failure. Failure would be if we sat back and did nothing, or revisited the same lesson from the previous year, which was the same lesson from the year before that. Unfortunately, many school environments do not see this as the reality—in many environments, the status quo is subconsciously encouraged by making it intensely difficult for entrepreneurially minded teachers to try new things. Schools are mired in bureaucracy and red tape, which is downright discouraging to someone who has redefined failure. After all, if nothing changes, nothing grows, and if nothing is growing, then due to the law of momentum, it is dying. But remember, there is no status quo, no limbo—we are either becoming better teachers or worse teachers, and building the entrepreneurial mindset guarantees growth and grit and the spirit of trying.

    Redefining failure means we cut certain words out of our vocabulary. Chief among these is the word "can't." Can't is a limited word—a word born out of fear and a word designed to keep our world as small as possible. Can't is, perhaps, the most abhorrent of four-letter words and those with the entrepreneurial mindset, who have successfully redefined failure, will avoid it at all costs. And yet our society pushes us into the state of "can't" to the point where it becomes our operating mentality—the reality of those who have been conditioned to fear not succeeding. After all, it is easier to say "no" than to say "why not?" but if we have the mindset of "why not?" and showcase this mindset to our students, the jump for them becomes second nature and before long, this becomes ingrained in their thinking as they push ever closer to thinking like an entrepreneur. And the truth is, thinking like an entrepreneur is far more exciting than responding in fear: Thinking like an entrepreneur means seeing possibility where there are problems, seeing alternatives where there are dead ends, seeing triumph where there is setback. Thinking like an entrepreneur means seeing the world in a way that is more exciting and full of wonder.

This does require balance. I am not suggesting we create an environment where mental strain and overall stress push us beyond our capacities—in fact, what I am suggesting is the opposite. Pushing ourselves by forging past obstacles will actually free us from the mental strain and stress of everyday life. It is this mental strain and stress that feeds into our mind and tells us we "can't" in the first place—this is the common state of the current high school student. She is not physically overstressed but is under mental strain from being pulled in far too many directions at once. She is overloaded with homework (some of which is little more than busywork), she has taken on too many extracurriculars (recommended by well-meaning adults who constantly point to her future college application), she is participating in three sports throughout the year each of which has practice for three to four hours a day, and she is trying to maintain relationships on top of everything else.

It's hard. But not "hard" in the "make you stronger" sense—it's hard in the break you down and wear you out sense. The entrepreneurial mindset, and specifically "redefining failure," demonstrates that there is nothing wrong with working hard (in fact this is how grit is developed) and effort should be embraced because this effort will teach us that *trying* is worth it. *Trying is how we discover the enormous range of our potential. Trying is how we redefine our capabilities and step out of the mold that we are limited.* We are, in fact, limitless—the only boundary on our success is our failure to dream as big as possible. As we move the concept of failure over to the realm of "not trying" we should also strive to see failure as not dreaming as big and as grandiose as possible. That's true failure—to accept a life of mediocrity and "average" when the entire universe is rallying for us to live as big and as full as possible.

This is the true entrepreneurial mindset—this is how we view the world not as a place of oppression and limitation but as a canvas for expression and fulfillment. And we do a disservice to our students when we box them in because we ourselves feel boxed in by administrations and assessments and parental expectations. It is ridiculous. We can never encourage students to overcome "can't" in their lives if we remain enslaved to the notion in our own lives. We must set the example, be the change, live the dream. We should be beyond average in our expectations of the everyday—when we wake up in the morning, we should, in every sense of the phrase, be ready to seize the day. We should be as excited as we expect our students to be, we should see the potential just waiting to be explored. Each day is a microcosm of our lives and if we want to live richly and deeply, we need to treat every day as a miracle.

When I work with schools on starting entrepreneurial programming with their students, I always start with the teacher in charge of the program. You can tell a lot about a person by asking them how they are doing. Are they down and out, are they living someone else's life? Are they currently in a job or are they fulfilling a calling? Are they living their best life or just going through the motions? This can quickly tell me whether a program will be successful—we must model the mindset we want our students to adopt, and this idea of redefining failure must be ingrained at our very core. And this is only possible once we have firmly established a growth mindset with a will to become grittier each and every day. Society wants us to accept failure as inevitable—as part of the consequence of living. We need to reject this—fling this idea far from our mind and accept that the only failure that exists is the failure when we refuse to try, when we dream too small, when we stay wrapped in our comfort. Anything else is a step forward on the path toward living the life we were meant to live.

Now imagine an entire program filled with teachers and students who think this way—now imagine what they *can* do when the word "can't" is not in their vocabulary.

STRATEGIES FOR REDEFINING FAILURE

Failure, in the traditional sense, cannot be planned. Failure, once it is redefined, can be avoided. If we look at failure as not trying in the first place, then our strategies for changing this mindset stem from getting students (and ourselves) to see possibility where there seems to be nothing but obstacles. Where others throw up their hands and say it's not possible, we look beyond to what could be. This is why the concept of *I can* must coincide with *I will*. It is not enough to admit that it is possible—though this is certainly the first battle. The main battle is to move past acceptance into action—once we commit to *I will*, we move into the trying phase and this is where we can move to avoid failure.

The issue is not the avoidance of failure—the issue is with the mindset of what failure really is. If we can condition ourselves to simply switch these definitions, then all of sudden we stop fearing the possibility of not succeeding and we start fearing the repercussions of not trying. This is the foundation of the entrepreneurial mindset. And it should not be wholly equated with risk-taking. Risk-taking has its place and it certainly is important and belongs in close relationship with the entrepreneurial mindset. But they are not two and the same. Risk-taking doesn't necessarily imply a cost-benefit analysis, or a carefully thought-out plan. There is, of course, an amount of risk-taking in all acts of trying, and without risk there would be no element of "not succeeding" (the traditional definition of failure). The point is, we can have an *I can, I will* attitude and not be labeled an extreme risk-taker because this attitude speaks more of confidence.

This is not the confidence of knowing the outcomes ahead of time. This is the confidence of knowing that no matter the outcome, it is better to try than not to try. This is the confidence born of experience and learning that the worst-case scenario is not necessarily that bad. This is the confidence learned the hard way, by asking someone out and getting rejected. That rejection can be overcome—what can't be is the never knowing what would have happened had you tried. This leads to a path of regret that lasts far longer than the sting of a refusal. Our strategy, then, must be to demonstrate to our students a clear acceptance of the redefinition of failure so that they are willing to accept the redefinition in their own lives.

How to do this is tricky because, like grit, this learning is taught more as a by-product. It is not possible to sit our students down and explain that all their lives what they have been calling "failure" is actually not failure. This sort of learning never sticks. Instead, like everything else in the entrepreneurial mindset, they must come to the realization themselves. Perhaps the greatest champion for this type of mindset is Richard Branson. The world-famous serial entrepreneur has shared his life's motto (and title of his autobiography) to the joy—and annoyance—of many. For Branson, one needs to adopt the philosophy of "Screw it, let's do it." In other words, we need to be willing to try. We need to be willing to say, here's an idea—could it work? Screw it, let's do it. Could this get us in trouble if it doesn't succeed? Screw it, let's do it. Is this worth taking a chance on? Screw it, let's do it.

Ingrain this style of thinking, and before long, the team will be operating with the mantra of "why not?" And this is a powerful mode of operation. Consider the story of Sean who, as an enterprising young seventh grader, sent me an email asking for a meeting. I was not really looking for an opportunity to have a meeting with a seventh grader without a clear purpose, so I inquired about the subject of the meeting. He replied, "I am presenting you with a fantastic opportunity."

Well now I was intrigued. We arranged the meeting, and we were joined by the assistant principal of the upper school. We sat down in the conference room in our seventh- and eighth-grade building, and Sean immediately set out his plan.

"Mr. Carter," he began, "we want to open a coffee bar here in our building modeled after The Leaning Eagle."

I said nothing as I let this soak in.

"We've discussed it as a team and we feel it would not only be successful, but it would also thrive."

I was stuck on the word "team"—this seventh-grade kid had already assembled a team for this idea?

"If you are willing, we would love your help in looking over the logistics of how this would work in our space. Would you be willing?"

A coffee bar with our seventh and eighth graders. Everything about this plan seemed wrong—what seventh and eighth graders drink coffee? How could the business sustain itself on roughly 20 percent of the potential customer base as the high school coffee bar? Was it unethical to serve caffeine to young students? Were they mature enough to run a business?

Questions about the infeasibility of the project rushed through my mind and everything pointed to this being a bad idea. But it was, after all, an idea. And an idea that had not only been introduced by a seventh grader but had been presented in an impressive, mature manner. Fortunately, I had already been deeply immersed in developing the entrepreneurial mindset by this point, so my reaction went straight to "Screw it, let's do it"—though I only said out loud the "let's do it" part.

Sean got to work with his team and before long, he was running a small but successful operation. Dubbed the "Mini Cup," this business soon pivoted into more snack-driven and began to grow and grow, year after year, until acquiring the funds through net revenue to build an impressive permanent location in one of the school's innovation spaces. The Mini Cup is now hailed as one of the core businesses of the entrepreneurship program and is a clear testament to the argument that students of any age, with dedication and effort, can run and operate a business. And to cap it off, there are multiple weeks a year when the sales from the Mini Cup exceed those of The Leaning Eagle.

Redefining failure is about trying. It's about applying growth mindset and armoring oneself with enough grit to take on challenges, and then not hesitating before saying, "Screw it, let's do it." And this is not to say that we do things just for the sake of doing them—there should still be a cost-benefit analysis with decisions, and there should still be questions and feedback and concerns. But our students need to see that success is possible and they need to develop the perseverance to work toward those long-term goals. This means understanding the crossroads. After they come up with the idea and do the research and figure out a potential path forward, they will come to a crossroads where a decision needs to be made—do they take the leap or stay on the safe side. This is where their learning needs to kick in—this is where they need to apply the redefinition of failure. They must lean on their training and choose to take the leap, embracing the unknown, armed with a plan, and ready to succeed, but be perfectly OK if it doesn't succeed.

It's also worth noting that this style of thinking runs contrary, in many ways, to the educational system. In education, we have put measures and systems in place to prevent, perhaps unintentionally, individuals from running off with ideas. Take the convoluted financial system present in many schools. It is all too common for a teacher who has an idea and even goes so far as to get the approval of the administration to then face down the bureaucratic task of getting the actual funding. They will be asked to fill out a PO and before they fill out a PO, they must track down any necessary forms ranging from W-9s to insurance paperwork to background checks. Once (and really *if*) they track down all these forms, then they must wait as long as two months before the PO is approved. Once approved, the process is not finished. Next, they must submit a payment request to actually get the funding—this payment request can only be submitted if the request is accompanied by the PO number that was issued and if the unsuspecting teacher did not include it, it is back to the drawing board. The payment request takes several weeks to process and once approved, kicks into gear the actual check writing, which takes another week or two (assuming the final invoice submitted has been revised to have a date *after* the date of the issued PO).

It's easy to see why many teachers, even ones with innovative ideas, give up in the ongoing frustration of jumping through hoops. And not only this, but the other systems in the school are still pulling at the teacher's time—they are still expected to respond to parent emails within twenty-four hours, to complete all grading in a "timely" manner, to attend faculty meetings, to submit lesson plans, and to craft engaging classroom activities. Then we wonder why teachers burn out. As the teachers are burning out before their eyes, the students also begin to burn out as they are pressured by society, by their parents, and by their school to achieve every possible accolade that would look good on a college resume by the time they are a high school junior. They join National Honor Society, they start clubs, they participate in three sports, they sing in the choir, they get a part in the school play, and they maintain a GPA of above a 4.0. And when we look into their empty, soulless eyes and see the lack of passion and interest, we wonder why.

The entrepreneurial mindset is about a reset. It's about going back to the basics and understanding what is important in life. It's about one's core values and staying true to those core values. It's about growth and grit and trying and opportunity. It's about developing a different outlook when all of society asks us to have the same outlook as everyone else. But this is where the mindset is freeing. When we open ourselves up to the "Screw it, let's do it" line of thinking, then obstacles no longer seem that big. In fact, we open ourselves up to creative ways around these obstacles—we think outside the box, we innovate and create and dream and then we pass that passion on to our students who innovate to create larger and dream bigger than we ever thought possible.

In 1993, David Bayles and Ted Orland published a book entitled *Art and Fear: Observations on the Perils (and Rewards) of Artmaking*. They told the story of an art teacher who wondered what would happen if he experimented with his assessment method. As a side note, consider the power (and it is powerful) of a teacher who wonders, "What would happen if?" Imagine the potential of asking not only "What if?" but also "Why not?" This teacher divided the room in half and assigned the first half to a quantity assessment and the second half to a quality assessment. The quantity side had to turn in fifty ceramic pots (any quality pot, even an atrocious one, was acceptable) to get an A while the quality side had only to turn in one perfect pot to get an A. At the end of the semester, the best works were turned in by the quantity group. Turns out, in working at something over and over, making attempt after attempt, a sort of refining process happens that yields a better result. Turns out, true failure has nothing to do with success and is rather the refusal to make attempt after attempt after attempt.

The impacts of this style of thinking on education are endless. Redefining failure is a key attribute of what is referred to as the entrepreneurial mindset. In enabling our teachers, and our students, to think like entrepreneurs—to ask, "What if?" and "Why not?"—we are giving them a path to success. A bumpy and misshapen path, for sure, but a path nonetheless where the learning yields not only rewards but a life free of inconsolable regret.

ATTRIBUTE FOUR: OPPORTUNITY SEEKING

Entrepreneurs are problem solvers—people who, by nature, seek to create solutions that cut to the center of an issue and solve it in innovative ways. Because of this, problems, to entrepreneurially minded people, are not obstacles as much as blessings. And this is a dramatic mindset shift. Once we shift this definition of "problem" from "something to get frustrated by and to cause us to shut down" toward "something to be embraced because it is really an opportunity," we have fully taken on the entrepreneurial mindset. While everyone else is paralyzed by the issue at hand, the entrepreneurially minded person is able to see the hidden blessing. Where everyone else sees a thunderstorm, they see the chance to sell umbrellas.

This does involve some careful rewiring of our thinking. Our brains are hardwired for survival, which usually means avoiding problems. If we can, over time, change this hardwiring so that we see these problems as something to be embraced, we will unlock a superpower. We may not be able to leap buildings and scale mountains, but the ability to see beyond the temporary displeasure of a "problem" is no less heroic. It is the stuff of motivational stories and inspiring books—it is the stuff of entrepreneurship. I started this book with the story of Caerus, and his spirit has permeated throughout. Caerus doesn't wait around for someone to notice him, nor does he linger with expectation. Caerus runs and he does not stop until we, without hesitation, grab his single lock of hair and hold fast. And this cannot happen unless we are ready, unless we are anticipating his presence.

Seizing opportunity doesn't just mean problem-solving—it means problem *seeking*. We need to get up, get out, and get looking for problems. Fortunately, problems are never hard to find. And when we see them as the opportunities they are, we are faced with the decision to chase them down or live with regret. We've all had those once-in-a-lifetime chances come our way only to pass on them and live with regret for years on end. Interestingly, the more we pass on the chances that come our way, the fewer and further between the chances become until, worn down by time, we become immune to opportunity and fully succumb to a reactive mindset.

Caerus works in curious ways. He will come running by once or twice and will give us a few chances to jump on board. But each time we refuse, he will keep running until someone else takes the leap. And the more someone else takes the leap, the more he will direct his path toward that person. Such is the case with serial entrepreneurs. Most of us live our lives waiting for "that one idea" that will change everything while serial entrepreneurs field idea after idea, seizing opportunity after opportunity, and meeting with mountains of success. We look at them as freaks of nature, as geniuses in their field, as oracles or a once-in-a-generation brainchild. In fact, they are just normal people who have conditioned themselves, year after year, to reach out for Caerus who they know now makes a dependable route and passes by regularly.

Sara Blakely paints an intriguing picture of the idea-seeking want-to-be-entrepreneur in her MasterClass on entrepreneurship. She shares her own vision of starting a company while not yet knowing what that company would be, even going so far as to "ask the universe" for direction and showcasing her willingness to embrace whatever idea was sent her way—that it would not be squandered. And because of this mindset, because of this opportunity seeking outlook, when she first cut the feet out of her pantyhose, she realized she was staring Caerus in the face. He went to run off, but she grabbed his hair and started an empire.

Ideas are not mystical. Ideas stem from problems, and problems abound in our society. With the right mindset, where there are problems, there are possibilities, and where there are possibilities, Caerus lurks just around the corner. It is advantageous for us to adopt this mindset to not only seize these opportunities but to live in a way that sees life as a gift, as a platform of opportunity to strive for whatever we want, rather than as an oppressive force bent on making us suffer. And if we can choose how to think, then we can seize every moment and make it count. Imbued with the entrepreneurial mindset, we will cherish the moments that make up our months and our years and our decades and, like Blakely, we will not squander our lives on petty, reactive thinking but rather invest our lives in the act of creating. We will work to make the world a better place because of our role in it.

The entire framework of the entrepreneurial mindset builds on the foundation established by growth mindset and grit. We can only truly redefine failure when we have the growth mindset and are willing to put forth the necessary effort, and we only become opportunity seeking at heart when we have the firm structure of the initial three attributes in place. One cannot be proactive if one is in a fixed mindset, and one cannot seize Caerus if one has no grit. This is why, in our academic programs as well in our faculty and staff as well as in our homes with our family, we should strive to champion this mindset. We should allow this mindset to permeate all that we do so that we can truly live our lives to the full and soak every bit of experience out of our finite time. If we willingly choose this mindset over and over, it will become part of how we think and we will truly embrace the life of the proactive person. And that is a rich life indeed.

OPPORTUNITY SEEKING STRATEGIES

At this point, you probably see a trend in these strategies—their effectiveness in our educational programming hinges entirely upon whether or not they are adopted by our faculty. As I travel to schools to conduct professional development, the starting point is always helping to establish these attributes with the administrators and the teachers so that they spill forth into every aspect of what we do with the students. Opportunity seeking works the same way—if we, as educators, reframe the way we view problems, our students will as well. After all, problems surround us and schools seem to offer up more problems than most institutions. This makes education the perfect canvas for fostering an opportunity seeking mindset.

It begins with an identity shift. Borrowing from James Clear's approach in *Atomic Habits,* changing a habit or moving toward a goal becomes clearer and more straightforward when we change our identity to match the intended result. In other words, stop saying you are going to go for a run and think of yourself as a *runner*. Stop stressing over the choices to eat healthy and think of yourself as *a healthy eater*. Stop saying you want to get up earlier and think of yourself as *a morning person*. Over time, this intentional shift will cause an entirely new identity to form that will propel you toward the habits necessary to accomplish the goals you've set.

Identify as a problem solver. Identify as someone who gets excited at the prospect of finding a problem because it may lead to the opportunity to solve it. This sort of identity is at the forefront of the linchpin or impact player in an organization. Want to make yourself indispensable? Start by shifting your identity. Once you start getting excited at finding a problem, you have created an entirely new mindset approach to one of the largest frustrations in life. You've given yourself a fundamental tool to rise above reactive thinking and fully embrace the benefits of being proactive. And as a by-product, you'll live a life that is happier with a greater sense of fulfillment and purpose. Even more, your students will recognize this.

One key strategy for becoming opportunity seeking is to create a problem funnel approach. This sort of approach has four distinct steps. Step one is to collect as many problems as possible—create a problem engine that enables you and your students to amass a tremendous list of problems. Begin by having your students brainstorm all the problems they have faced so far that day. Go from waking up (not wanting to get out of bed, oversleeping, missing breakfast, late for school, traffic issues, fighting over what music to listen to on the way to school, sibling issues, and so on) to the first several classes of the day (too many quizzes, not enough time to finish homework, social issues, always hungry, teacher wouldn't let you go use the bathroom, too tired to focus) to lunch and afternoon classes (forgot credit card and couldn't get lunch, wasn't able to sit with friends during lunch, got called out during class for drawing) to afterschool and extracurriculars (forgot shoes for practice and had to call mother, raining and got all wet, sick of having to run sprints, still don't have a date for homecoming) and so on throughout the day. The problem engine will generate at least ten to twenty problems per day, every day, and many times these will be recurring problems that are faced every day.

Collect these problems with enthusiasm and excitement knowing that the more problems you collect, the more opportunities you now have to demonstrate an entrepreneurial mindset. Remember, you are now a problem solver. Encourage your students to think this way as well Consider placing a problem engine box in a visible place in the school and ask people to write down their most frustrating problems and put them in the box. Automate the system even further with a QR code and some sort of incentive for the best overall problem (maybe a gift card to one of your student-run businesses). Although they'll end up with lots of ridiculous problems, your students will start to discover trends and see patterns in the types of problems their fellow students face. Once they've identified a fair number of these, it's time to start customer surveys. Customer surveys are useful for several reasons, but one primary benefit is that helps students identify "customer pain points." Solve this problem, and the result is a satisfied customer. Solve this problem for a whole group of customers, and you've got a business concept. As has often been said, if you want to be a millionaire, solve a problem for a million people. If you want to be a billionaire, solve a billion-person problem. And so on.

This involves getting our students to follow the problem-solving engine from their own problems to the problems of others. Along the way, they will begin developing empathy (another by-product of opportunity seeking) as they start with what they know (their own problems) and then venture to the people they know (their first customer base) until finally encountering the problems of the people they don't know. And all of this hinges on helping students reframe how they see problems. After a while, they will start to get excited when problems surface. Not only will this make for a great path to entrepreneurial thinking, but it will also make for a far more enjoyable life for the student—a life of seeing problems as something positive is a life that will be lived well. As educators, it is truly a high calling to help develop this mindset in our students.

But collecting the problems is only the first step; next you must send the problems through the first filter. This filter exists in the same realm as the famous "Serenity Prayer." In this scenario, the speaker implores God to grant us "the serenity to accept the things [we] cannot change, the courage to change the things [we] can, and the wisdom to know the difference." For this filter, take one of the problems and ask yourself, is this a problem within my power to change? Yes or no? Any problems that seem within your power to change go on to the next step. Any that are not in your power to change get tossed in the recycling bin—these problems, by the way, are problems that often we just have to get over. If it is not in our power to change, then it ought not be something we complain about.

Soon, after sending these problems through the first filter, you'll have eliminated those not worth considering and given yourself clarity around key problems of focus. This is where the third step takes place. Each problem now needs to be looked at with the following question in mind: Does solving this problem directly contribute to my *why*? This is a game changer. If we have taken the time (in our work on growth mindset) to clearly establish our mission, vision, and values, we now have a premade filter to supercharge our opportunity seeking skills. If we chase after every single problem that is within our power to solve, we will be going in a hundred directions at once and our growth will be unfocused and our lives will be chaotic. Instead, we must return to our starting point and ask if solving this problem will help us with our vision and allow us to live out our core values.

When working with a group of students, this becomes equally as important. If, perhaps, we are preparing to launch a venture at the school, we must first clarify *why* we are launching this venture and then figure out the problem the venture is trying to solve before then landing at the customer who is experiencing the problem we are solving. This sort of approach allows us to keep purpose at the forefront and not follow every shiny problem down an unending rabbit hole. Once we determine, however, that a problem does in fact help us live out our *why*, then the final step comes into play: take action.

This is the step that separates the doers from the talkers. This is the step that clearly establishes those who think with an entrepreneurial mindset: Entrepreneurs are action-biased and when in doubt, they do it. They don't sit around and map out each and every potential scenario and they don't wait around for all sorts of signs and suggestions. Instead, they collect problems, determine if they are solvable, determine if they warrant their focus, and then they act. Simple but profound—the core of the opportunity seeking attribute. Jim Rohn, famous speaker, writer, and mentor of many, urges in much of his work that we must not "let [our] learning lead to knowledge—let it lead to action." The downfall of many well-meaning educator is to stop at the knowledge phase and not take the next step into action, but it is this step where every attribute of the entrepreneurial mindset hinges—everything has led to this moment and everything is poised on this key identifiable action.

And in the classroom, taking action is fun. This involves moving from the collecting and sifting phase into the ideation phase—the actual problem-solving. You have identified which problems are worth solving and now you can find which ones the students spark to. In the ideation stage, they create a series of potential solutions to the problem at hand. In the beginning, encourage outlandish solutions. There is no such thing as a "bad" solution. Every and anything goes. For example, consider the difficulty the average teenager has waking up in the morning. Every time we have conducted a problem engine at CHCA, this problem has surfaced as one of the top ones, a true customer pain point. When we begin the ideation stage, inevitably the goofiest of ideas will surface: an alarm clock that releases the smell of bacon and a bed that gradually inclines to a sitting position, to name two. After the ridiculous ideas are out in the open and after the students see that these ideas are not greeted with ridicule and shame, the truly great ones begin to surface.

We've dreamed up smart mirrors that help students pick out outfits (Cher's closet in *Clueless* for those of us who remember the '90s), refrigerators that scan items for calorie count and expiration dates, preheated shower dials to minimize time waiting for water to heat up, adjustable dumbbells with built-in metrics for tracking workouts, umbrellas that connect to iPhones and include speakers, and plenty more. While most of these ideas are far from feasible or have an incredibly narrow potential customer base, they build in students the natural sense of opportunity seeking. No matter the problem (can't figure out what to wear, food doesn't get used and goes bad, workouts are hard to track, and the ongoing issue of weather), it demonstrates that solutions can be found.

It's also worth pointing out that much of this stage of the entrepreneurial journey is an intellectual exercise. It is certainly worth entertaining the idea of a *Shark Tank*-style accelerator where students pitch a variety of these concepts, but by and large, these won't make for solid student-run businesses at your school. And that's fine—you're not in this exercise to generate business ideas, you're in it to demonstrate the mindset and this mindset, once developed, will lead to more businesses, dripping with success, than you could ever hope to manage. And occasionally, it just works out. Consider our wood-fired pizza concept. The primary problem was that we needed money to finish the building of the teaching kitchen. The secondary problem (and the one that fit our customer pain point) was that students had practice after school and often were hungry by 3 p.m. A pain point we didn't even anticipate was that teachers, on Fridays, were less likely to want to go home and cook dinner for their family after a long week and more likely to eat out. This desire to eat out led them to buy multiple pizzas from our wood-fired pizza oven to then take home and feed the family.

And this illustrates an important point about opportunity seeking and problem-solving—often the problem you are setting out to solve is not the problem you end up solving. And this is good—great, even. The problem you ended up solving is probably one you never anticipated in the first place and never would have discovered had you been too afraid to try. In the end, seeking opportunity is about much more than grabbing a lock of hair—it is about reimagining the nature of problems, it is about embracing adversity, it is about seeing the potential in every issue. It's about understanding other people and it's about trying to make the world a better place. If we accept that the world is not perfect and exists in a broken state, then the act of bringing wholeness is itself a spiritual act. This elevates opportunity seeking beyond a classroom exercise and into another realm entirely—this makes problem-solving the stuff of life and provides us with not only purpose but hope. This makes us move ever closer to embracing the entrepreneurial mindset.

It also helps us develop skills to sharpen existing situations. Consider the example of Eagle Farms from several years ago—during the immediate aftermath of COVID, produce sales from our e-commerce platform soared. We could barely keep up with the weekly orders and were consistently running out of products that customers wanted. Then, slowly, over time, orders began to wane more and more until only a small trickle remained. This clearly was a problem. With the entrepreneurial mindset, however, it was also an opportunity.

As a team, we approached the problem by using the previously mentioned "five whys" technique. The technique suggests that the root cause of any problem can be found by drilling down through the continuous asking of the word *why*. We started with the obvious and the first *why*.

"*Why* are sales down in Eagle Farms?" I asked.

"Because people aren't buying the produce," the students said.

"*Why* aren't people buying the produce," I asked.

"Because they don't know about it. My own mom doesn't even know about how to order it. Most of the parents don't know, only a few," said one young lady in the class.

"*Why* don't the parents at the school know about the business," I asked.

"I don't know," the students said. "I guess because they don't hear about it."

"*Why* don't they hear about it?" I asked.

At this point it is worth pointing out that this exercise, when done with students, can be tedious and a bit annoying so it must be handled with a tongue-in-cheek approach so as to get to the root cause without causing too much eye-rolling.

"They should hear about it," one young woman said. "After all, we post on social media about it."

"Yeah," another student said, "we post all the time, we are always posting."

Here I deviated slightly from the *why* questions to get to the heart of the issue.

"What social media platforms are we posting on?" I asked.

"TikTok," they said immediately. "And Instagram. We have a lot of followers."

"Can we pull up a list of followers?" I asked.

The students whipped out their phones and began scrolling through over a hundred names.

"How many of those followers are parents?" I asked.

The students continued scrolling.

"Not many," one student offered up in response a few moments later.

"Hmm," I said. "Just out of curiosity, what social media do your parents use?"

"Facebook," they said without missing a beat. "The moms are on Facebook and the dads are on LinkedIn."

The last *why* didn't even need to be asked at this point—the revelation was clear. Of course the parents didn't know about it because the marketing had been directed to other classmates through Instagram pictures taken amid our twenty-foot-tall vertical tomatoes and our aeroponic towers bursting with green. The TikTok videos had been, admittedly, quite funny and inventive and designed purely to get likes from fellow classmates.

And the parents remained unreached.

I often draw the connection between this sort of root cause problem-solving and the act of weeding a garden. This is an act our students are all too familiar with as our campus features multiple growing areas that, while often beautiful, require an extreme amount of attention through weeding. And, not surprisingly, this is perhaps one of the hardest activities to convince students to embrace with an optimistic attitude. More often than not, the students move through the zones of the garden, lightly grabbing the weeds from the surface and pulling the leaves while leaving the roots firmly behind, embedded in the soil. As anyone with gardening experience knows, this is a futile act. Days later, the weeds will be back and often stronger than before simply because the problem was tackled from the surface level and not the root cause.

When we approach problems not from the standpoint of frustration or even paralysis but rather with the excitement inherent in the opportunity seeking mindset, we reframe the entire nature of the situation. We become energized by the hunt for solutions and we use tools, like the five whys, that apply not only in this circumstance but to all problems we will face later in life. And tools like this help us live lives of empowerment where we realize that attacking the root cause eradicates the problem in a way that surface-level thinking never does.

In the end, opportunity seeking is a core attribute in the entrepreneurial mindset but it is an attribute that requires a foundation below it that is structurally solid. This foundation is built on growth mindset that fuels our actions with purpose and direction. This foundation continues with grit, which gives us the passion and the perseverance necessary to accomplish our long-term goals. This foundation is further strengthened by the redefining of failure and the coming to understand that true failure is not trying in the first place. If these attributes are in place, then opportunity seeking becomes the launch pad from which the rockets of innovation can take off, soar, and reach unimaginable heights not just in the classroom but in all of life. Let's embrace this mindset if for no other reason than to empower our students to pilot these rockets into frontiers we cannot even begin to comprehend—that is a legacy worth leaving.

FINAL CHARGE

We live in a dichotomy. Our culture is moving toward normalizing isolation as we fully explore the potential of remote work. The pandemic pushed us closer toward the reality of living and working independent of in-person communities and DoorDash has now made it possible to enjoy restaurant dining without even leaving the house. This is nothing compared to the isolation created by the digital age of smartphones as more and more studies link anxiety and mental strain to the continuous use of devices. The dichotomy comes into play as we continue to strive for meaningful relationships in the face of this increasing isolation. As we become more alone, we push for more community. And this community is important—not just for the mental benefits of living life with others, but also for the tribal benefit of understanding commonalities of human experience. Without a community, we are living lives of solitude that continuously push us to question our purpose and meaning. Without a clearly defined purpose and meaning, we meander aimlessly throughout life and often take our existence for granted. And as bad as it may be for us, the effects are far worse on our young adults. We have yet to fully understand the ramifications of just two years of quarantining and remote requirements, much less the social effects of what has happened in the years since things have, mostly, gone back to "normal."

We need, more than ever, to embrace an entrepreneurial mindset. An entrepreneurial mindset, by its nature, is a community-minded way of thinking that takes other people into account. After all, without customers, there is no entrepreneur. Without problems, there are no solutions, and without opportunities, there is no need to apply growth mindset, grit, and redefining failure. The natural outgrowth of the entrepreneurial mindset finds its primary purpose and culmination in the act of empathy and in effectively communicating this empathy to others. The final stage of entrepreneurial thinking occurs when, armed with the core attributes of entrepreneurship, the individual encounters, often for the first time, the realization that there are others in the universe and that their problems merit solving therefore presenting opportunities for those who seize them. Empathy, after all, is not feeling sorry for other people but *feeling* for other people, acknowledging that they exist and seeing the world from their perspective. It is epitomized in the final scene of Harper Lee's *To Kill a Mockingbird* when Scout Finch realizes that all along, her father was right: "You never really know a man until you stand in his shoes and walk around in them." We could all stand to do a little more of that.

Even the simple act of communication can be difficult for our students—more and more, they have been stripped of every opportunity to talk directly, face-to-face, to others and many times they come across as terrified to do so. They want to merely google the thoughts of others, or outsource the conversation to a survey on social media, but the only way to really convince them that other people exist is to get them out of their comfort zone and into a situation where they have to communicate. Talking to humans is important for many reasons but if nothing else, it leads to the development of empathy. And empathy helps lay the foundation for generosity.

Now, when it comes to generosity, we face an interesting dilemma. The bulk of exposure that our students get to entrepreneurship comes from social media. From influencers on TikTok to twenty-something millionaires on Instagram to *Shark Tank* celebrities to reality show winners, we are inundated with tales of people who skyrocketed to fame and fortune from a single idea that went viral. As a result, our students' view of entrepreneurship is framed with achieving celebrity stardom and riches. Often, students come into my class excited about entrepreneurship as they express their desire to make billions of dollars. When pressed on why they want to do this, they say it is to retire early. When asked why they want to retire early, they explain, after a pause, that they just want to live on a beach somewhere.

"And then what?"

"Well, I don't know," they say. "I guess just do whatever I want."

"And what's that—what would you do if you could do whatever you want?"

"I don't know. I guess hang out with my friends and stuff."

The issue isn't that they want to make tons of money—the issue is they don't know why. They are separated from the power of purpose, of calling, and they have fallen for the trap of sensation. They think that by gaining the world, they will gain significance and meaning, but the irony is that, in their attempt to gain the world, they will lose their entire sense of purpose. In the end, it is strategies around empathy and generosity that help us achieve our sense of meaning. Many of us have chosen education as our profession primarily to drive meaningful impact in the lives of others—we have connected our work to a greater purpose. The same is true for the billionaires who give their wealth away for greater causes—meaningful impact. This is the power of generosity. A friend and founding member of our school community often says that one of the most powerful callings we may have is to help separate people from their wealth. If it is for a noble and honorable cause, how much better to be generous. This is the lesson we honor through our constant reimagining of Charles Dickens's *A Christmas Carol*—moving from hoarding wealth to being generous with wealth is a healthy and life-altering transformation.

Why not start this mindset when we are young? After all, they say it is much easier to begin the habit of being generous when we don't have much to be generous with than when we have much to give away. It is often thought that it will be easy to be generous when one is wealthy, but this thinking doesn't consider the sheer difficulty of giving away large amounts of money if there is not a preestablished habit of doing so. Helping students understand the core value of empathy is then key to establishing a generous mindset—and this is all connected back to entrepreneurship. If our true goal is to solve a problem for another person, then the monetary reward is second (or possibly even third) to the inner joy of having made the world a better place. Famous motivational speaker Zig Ziglar is known for his constant refrain: "You can have everything you want in life if you help enough other people get what they want." The truth in this statement derives from empathy, which then leads to generosity, empathy's outgrowth. Author and professor Brené Brown argues that empathy drives connection and is therefore far removed from sympathy, which drives disconnection. Empathy, she says, is "feeling *with* people." It is about understanding that what makes something better is a point of connection and if we truly enter that space, we find ourselves living out generous lives.

It is worth saying that once we make the conscious choice to live out the entrepreneurial mindset, life will not simply be peachy keen. We are consciously choosing discomfort, and growth, and grit over the easy route. Because of this, obstacles begin to manifest. Everything will seem to go wrong. The funding will fall through, the arrangement of class bells will prove to be a hassle, coworkers we thought were on our side will turn against us, we will experience challenges from parents, and students will flake out. And all of this will be a chance for us to test our resolve—how serious are we about this mindset? How serious are we about using roadblocks as chances to test our opportunity seeking ability? If this is nothing more than a chance to start a flashy new educational program or be able to use the word *innovative*, then now is the time to bow out. This type of shift requires full commitment and forward momentum despite obstacles and difficulties. This is not for the weak of heart or small of mind. Steve Harvey has said that the quickest way to kill a big dream is to tell it to a small-minded person. In this scenario, we must embrace the big dream wholeheartedly and run from the small-minded person just as wholeheartedly. This is about our survival as much as it is about the survival of our students.

In running it's referred to as hitting the wall. That moment in the race when the spectators vanish and you find yourself alone, feet pounding the pavement, lungs beating in your chest, and you begin to question your *why*. Athletes prepare for this, anticipating the wall and steeling themselves to bulldoze through it (or, even better, vault over it). We educators are not given the same level of training. Sure, we have guest speakers and professional development, but we aren't necessarily equipped to handle the "hit you in the face" brutality of the uphill climb. And it becomes worse when the uphill climb feels unending day after day.

As a result, it can often be tempting to not climb at all. After all, when we stay at the bottom of the mountain, the weather is usually calm, the food is plentiful, and the wildlife is tamer. We don't have to worry about the trek down, and we can relax and do as much deep breathing as we would like. But as we also know, the scenic views and take-our-breath-away experiences only come from making it to the top of the mountain—we'll never get the adrenaline rush from staying at base camp. We must be careful, though, to distinguish the true climb from the whirlwind. The whirlwind, also known as the email inbox, the parent-teacher meetings, the staff meetings, the parent-teacher-staff meetings, or really any meeting whatsoever, can feel, at times, exhilarating in its intensity. It brings with it the illusion of mountain climbing. After all, the wind is whipping all around us and we feel as if we are making incredible progress. But what the whirlwind leaves us with, after the dust has settled, is the stark realization that we're still at our starting point except noticeably more exhausted.

If we are to climb to great heights and ascend the mountain, we need to move out of the whirlwind and start the true uphill climb. But we must do this with the knowledge that the journey will bring with it not one, not two, but countless walls. And with each wall, we will question our *why*, and search for what may be nonexistent inner strength. This is the burden we must carry when we create something new and find ourselves pursuing a bigger *why*. And to succeed, we must train for the walls. We must anticipate the walls; we must go so far as to seek them out just to develop the grit and tenacity needed to prove to ourselves that the wall will not stop us. It may slow us down and it may give us pause, but it will not make us give up. And that is because in the distance, we can see the peak. It will be shrouded in clouds, but it will be there nonetheless. And we must remind ourselves that the peak is worth it—that reaching the summit is bigger than the wall and the frustration and the daily grind and the beating that we endure when we strive for something bigger.

In short, we must prepare for the inevitability of obstacles. For the coworkers who will complain about us both behind our backs and to our faces. For the administrators who bury us in busy work and then wonder why we are not reaching for the stars. For the parents who smother their children with watchful expectation while expecting us to do the parenting for them. For the emails, and the meetings, and the to-do lists, and everything that requires our attention and distracts us from our climb. It is in these moments that our own grit is developed, and it is in these moments that we find the strength that will carry us to great heights in the coming years. And it is in these moments that we discover if our *why* is big enough. If it is, in fact, a calling.

Calling is an interesting word—we spend a considerable amount of time dissecting it in our entrepreneurship program.

Calling suggests something higher, something bigger. Calling seems to imply a *why*. Most often, as educators, we are preparing students for a job, or, at best, for work. The question is what would it take to prepare students for a calling? What would it take to imbue them with a purpose-driven pursuit to go out and find that which they were created to do? How can we justify sitting back and relaxing while graduating class after graduating class continues to go out into cookie-cutter majors at safe institutions to prepare for "careers" in fields not of their own choosing? If we are *called* to be educators, we are also called to be guides and mentors. Our calling is no small one indeed—we are to work tirelessly to guide students to their purpose.

And sometimes we can get sidetracked by passion. We spend a lot of time encouraging students to discover and pursue a passion, explaining that this is the key to a life of happiness and satisfaction. Cal Newport, computer science professor at Georgetown University, has debunked this ideology in showing that it can be more damaging to one's sense of fulfillment and purpose if one is focused solely on finding and exploring one's passion. This sort of thinking leads to leaving job after job in pursuit of the one thing he/she was meant to do. Newport suggests that, instead, we should be focused on building and developing "career capital," which is developed by bringing a sense of excellence to one's work over a period of time in order to fully become irreplaceable.

This sort of thinking falls more squarely in line with the entrepreneurial mindset. We are not necessarily teaching students to jump on a motorcycle and ride across the country in search of their purpose and we are not necessarily encouraging them to spend months in Nepal seeking enlightenment. While these pursuits may be rewarding to some, they do not demonstrate a sustainable track toward career capital. Instead, we should be encouraging students to look at work not as meaningless labor but as a path toward a calling. We are called not to aimlessly churn out widgets as part of a cog in a larger machine but to think and act creatively, bringing innovation together with ideation to make the world a better place. This type of work brings inherent purpose and will fuel our fulfillment in life.

This is the sort of work that will, in essence, not feel like work and will lead toward a life well lived. This is not about where one is working but it is about the mindset with which one is working. With the right mindset, a manager of a restaurant will be fulfilling a calling as much as an entrepreneur leading a tech start-up. This mindset will prepare our students to thrive no matter where life takes them and will teach them that the path toward satisfaction and fulfillment is through growth mindset, grit, redefining failure, opportunity seeking, generosity, empathy, and effective communication. This doesn't mean working hard solely for the sake of working hard, nor does it mean embracing a life of ease solely to embrace a life of ease. It means pouring oneself into good work with the understanding that one's work is a reflection of one's life and one's purpose and one's sense of meaning. It means reclaiming the joy of work and giving the next generation the chance to live a truly beautiful life.

I close with a secular prayer for the entrepreneur in us all:

> *May we understand our why and allow it to guide our direction in life.*
>
> *May we embrace a lifelong sense of balanced growth and let it infuse all we do.*
>
> *May we resolve to face difficulty and obstacles with grit and determination to succeed.*
>
> *May we set long-term goals and chase them down with passion and perseverance.*
>
> *May we take risks and try new things once we have redefined what it means to fail.*
>
> *May we get up, get out, and set about living life by taking action.*
>
> *May we see a broken world not as a mess of problems but as a sea of opportunities.*
>
> *May we observe the world from the perspective of others and live life generously.*
>
> *May we, in essence, live life through developing the entrepreneurial mindset.*

MISSION, VISION, VALUES

It took a full ten-year journey for the Entrepreneurship and Sustainability Program to come to the point of fully realizing its mission, its vision, and its values. From the beginning, the drivers of success included a laser-like focus on increasing student engagement while striving for excellence. Along the way, as has been detailed in the previous pages, the core attributes of the entrepreneurial mindset were discovered. Along the way, an innovative approach to education was discovered.

This fall, 2023, I stood in a conference room addressing the Entrepreneurship and Sustainability team. Our team, ever growing in size, now includes a full-time program director, a full-time associate director, a full-time lead program manager, a full-time small business lead teacher, a full-time culinary instructor, a full-time horticulture program manager, a part-time wellness coach, and a part-time marketing and sales teacher. Ever the proponent of reflection, I thought back to several years ago when the burgeoning program had but one instructor. I smiled and set about the task of casting the vision for the immediate year and the years to come.

Vision casting is now one of my primary areas of focus along with taking our mission and infusing it into our values-based team culture. All in all, I was on fire for the launch of this most exciting school year. And part of the reason was the clarity around our *why*.

I was excited to share our mission, our vision, and our values, or more specifically, to share why we exist, where we are going, and what we stand for.

MISSION

When asked why we do what we do, we proudly exclaim that **we exist to develop the entrepreneurial mindset in all learners**. When asked why that matters, we explain that this mindset allows them **to be radically transformed to impact their lives**. And through this, to impact their **families**, their **churches**, their **communities**, their **workplaces**, and **every sphere of life** in which they find themselves.

We believe the entrepreneurial mindset is comprised of **growth mindset, grit, redefining failure**, and **opportunity seeking**, and that we are called to develop this thinking in **all learners**—students, parents, teachers, administrators, business owners, and everyone we can possibly reach.

VISION

When asked where we are going, we explain that this style of education, based firmly on **engaging learners with hands-on, innovative experiences that provide practical training for success in life** will revolutionize traditional education. We go on to say, with much enthusiasm, that we are part of a movement to create **meaningful, impactful opportunities** for students to develop the tools that will carry them to unbelievable heights.

We say, in short, that the sky is not the limit because those who think like entrepreneurs venture out into an ever-expanding universe of possibilities.

VALUES

As a team focused on driving student engagement toward the benchmark of excellence in all we do, we operate from the following core values:

1. **We align with our messaging** (we each demonstrate the attributes of the entrepreneurial mindset in all circumstances)
2. **We create unforgettable moments** (seeking to blow people away with our dedication to excellence)
3. **We are curious** (always learning, always seeking to answer the question "what if?")
4. **We recognize, affirm, and uplift** (in order to create a positive, optimistic space in which we can fulfill our calling)
5. **We help each other** (without having to be asked and without a begrudging spirit)

Armed with the clarity that direction brings, it only makes sense to share the two words that closed our opening day and ushered in our opportunity-charged school year:

LET'S GO!

ABOUT THE AUTHOR

Stephen Carter is the director of entrepreneurship and sustainability at Cincinnati Hills Christian Academy in Cincinnati, OH where he has taught for the last seventeen years. Under Stephen's direction, the program has grown from a single, student-run business into a full academic program with six student-managed businesses and over fifteen elective courses serving hundreds of students in grades K-12.

His mission is to develop the entrepreneurial mindset in all learners so they are radically transformed to impact their lives. He focuses his attention on the attributes of growth mindset, grit, redefining failure, and opportunity seeking while helping students engage in hands-on, innovative education that provides practical training for success in life.

His first book, which teaches financial literacy to young adults through a fable format, was published in 2021, and he has since embarked on helping K-12 schools develop entrepreneurship programming. Through his company, Seed Tree Group, Stephen offers consulting, speaking, and coaching services to K-12 schools. His expertise in creating entrepreneurship programming that is specific to a school's mission, vision, and values has enabled successful start-up programs around the nation. He also conducts professional development at schools to help teachers and administrators develop an "intrapreneurial mindset" so they can more effectively teach entrepreneurial concepts.

When he's not speaking, developing curriculum, or teaching classes on entrepreneurship, Stephen can be found spending time with his family while pursuing his ever-growing list of hobbies.

NEXT STEPS

Ready to Take the Entrepreneurial Mindset to the Next Level?

Visit www.seedtreegroup.com or email Stephen directly at Stephen@Seedtreegroup.com to find out how...

CONSULTING

SPEAKING

COACHING

At your school can radically transform your administrators, teachers, students, and parents to further develop their entrepreneurial mindset.